The GREEDY BLINDERS

RECIPE BOOK

This edition published in 2020
By SJG Publishing, HP22 6NF, UK

Cover design: Milestone Creative
Layout: seagulls.net
Recipes editor: Isobel Tupman

ISBN: 978-1-913004-12-5

Printed in China

10 9 8 7 6 5 4 3 2 1

Contents

Introduction

If you've watched the TV series *Peaky Blinders*, you'll be all too familiar with the dark, brooding settings of the English city of Birmingham and the Black Country in the post-First World War period. But did you know that the Peaky Blinders were based on an actual gang? They – along with rival gangs – were a very real part of the lawless, wild backstreets of Birmingham from the late 1800s to the 1930s, leaving a trail of crime and destruction in their wake.

The success of the TV series has ignited a fascination with the late 19th and early 20th century period and a renewed interest in all things Brum and Black Country. And that includes the 'fittle' (food). This recipe book will take you around the backstreets with traditional dishes from the stomping grounds of the Blinders, peppered with fascinating facts about the history, the food and, of course, the real gangsters and thugs of the time. Plus, you'll find a tasty selection of universal favourites with a rough and tumble gangster twist.

So, arm yourself with utensils, get the flames going and start cooking up a feast, Greedy Blinders style!

Who Were The Real Peaky Blinders?

Head back to the period that stretches from the late 19th century to the two decades after the First World War and you'll find an England steeped in industrialism and economic hardship amongst the working classes. With people struggling to make ends meet, it was the perfect breeding ground for gangs, with members doing anything to better their position, even if it meant violence, risk of prison and potential death.

The Peaky Blinders were a street gang based in and around Birmingham. It was made up of young men – sometimes as young as 12 – mostly from the lower to middle classes. They got their money, status and their kicks from robbery, illegal bookmaking, racketeering and generally being violent and exceedingly unpleasant.

– WHY 'PEAKY'? –

It wasn't because they'd all eaten something dodgy! At the time, 'peaky' referred to any flat hat with a peak. This style was the headwear of choice for the gang and gave them a distinctly dapper look. (For more on their sartorial style, see Dressing for a Dapper Dinner on page 33.) Story has it that they sewed razor blades into the peaks so that the caps could be used as weapons. However, many say this is a myth – disposable razor blades weren't even available when the gangs first emerged in the 1890s.

– WHY 'BLINDERS'? –

There are two main theories as to where 'blinders' came from. It was said that if a gang member headbutted someone, the razor sewn into their cap would cut their victim and blood would run into their eyes, thus 'blinding' them. A great story (and fantastic for drama on screen) but we know that the razor-in-the-peak weapon was probably no more than that – a story.

The other – and perhaps more plausible – theory is that the Peaky Blinders would sneak up behind a victim and pull the victim's own hat down over their eyes so that they couldn't identify who had attacked or robbed them.

– WHAT HAPPENED TO – THE PEAKY BLINDERS?

All good – and, in this case, bad – things must come to an end and, by the late 1910s, the Peaky Blinders were fading away. Their influence and control in the criminal underworld was usurped by the Birmingham Boys Gang and the infamous Sabini family.

But their influence lingers on. The term 'blinder' is still used today in Brummie slang to describe someone of a well-groomed, stylish appearance.

– CRIME AND – PUNISHMENT

As Britain industrialised, crime rates soared. From the TV series, it looked like gangs ran free with little intervention from the police – apart from the imposing presence of the evil Inspector Chester Campbell of course (who was based on a real-life chief constable brought into Birmingham in 1899 in response to growing brutality towards the police). The Blinders *et al* doled out their own brutal justice and retribution.

The temperance movement and anti-alcohol reform were widespread throughout the 19th century. In the 1870s, drunkenness became a big problem and a policeman could expect to bring in tens of drunks on a Saturday night. It seemed that eating was second place to drinking! And it wasn't just the men being corrupted by alcohol - 'shebeening' (selling alcohol without a licence) was one crime committed by more women than men.

As Britain moved into the Edwardian era in 1901, violent crime was seen to be falling. However, less serious crimes – such as petty theft and drunkenness – were still on the rise. At the turn of the century, imprisonment was the commonest form of punishment and could include hard labour. Juvenile offenders could be sent to reformatories or industrial schools (which were replaced by borstals in 1908). Common crimes for children aged between 9 and 13 were theft, hanging around with thieves, being beyond parental control (!) and truancy.

– PRISON GRUB –

If you were sent to prison, you could expect to be eating revolting food. And this was by design – there were no luxuries afforded to you by the authorities. (Prison reform in the 19th century made some improvements, but it remained a pretty horrible place to find yourself.) Prison food was designed simply to keep you alive, not to be enjoyed! The shorter your sentence, the worse you were fed. Here are some of the delights you could expect to eat:

Bread

Gruel – a thin porridge, made with oat, wheat, or rye flour and boiled in water or milk

Hard, flavourless **cheese**

Stirabout – something even worse and more tasteless than gruel! Made with cornmeal, oatmeal and salt

Suet – served as a meat substitute. You weren't expecting to actually eat meat were you? If you were a man doing hard labour you might get a small amount, but women and children were rarely given meat. Suet is made from rendered fat from around the kidneys of an animal. It was also used more generally in puddings and pastries but prisoners certainly wouldn't have been served this more flavoursome form of suet!

Potatoes

Milk – unfortunately, Victorian milk often contained boracic acid to keep it from souring. Boracic acid often caused nausea, vomiting and diarrhoea. Plus, it was unpasteurised, which meant it could gift you additional nasties.

Blinding Breakfasts

Breakfast As We Know It

In the mid 19th century, a breakfast for the wealthier Victorians would have consisted of cold meats, cheese and beer. (Yes, beer!) This was gradually replaced by porridge, fish, bacon and eggs.

What we know as the Full English Breakfast grew in popularity in the Victorian era (for the workers as well as the wealthier Victorians) and retained that popularity until the 1950s. However, by the end of the 19th century, sugary breakfast cereals started to take over.

One name of course springs immediately to mind: Dr John Harvey Kellogg. Now, this is something you won't read on the official Kellogg's website: it is said that Dr Kellogg created cornflakes as a healthy way to prevent masturbation (a subject he was apparently fixated on). He believed that by replacing bacon and eggs with a more bland breakfast food – cornflakes – it would lead to less 'excitement' in young men. Yes, Dr Kellogg had some very strange views on sex and other topics! (This isn't the first time breakfast has been thought sinful. In the Middle Ages in England, very few of the masses ate breakfast. The Catholic church leaders considered that eating too soon in the day was the sin of gluttony.)

A big boost to breakfasts – especially the 'full English' – came in 1886 when Heinz Tomato Ketchup was launched in the UK, followed by HP Brown Sauce in 1903.

Black pudding has also been making a massive resurgence in recent years. Some argue that black pudding originates from Scotland and shouldn't therefore be part of the 'full English'. But hungry breakfast customers tend to think otherwise and the customer is always right!

Brummie Bacon Cakes

Great for hangovers if you've been out for whiskey with the gang the night before, these bacon cakes are sure to sort you out and set you up for the day ahead. Hailing from Birmingham, these delicious savoury scones can be served hot or cold, spread with butter or served with other breakfast staples, such as eggs and tomatoes.

– INGREDIENTS –
Makes 8 cakes

3 rashers streaky bacon
(smoked or unsmoked – choose your weapon!)

225g sieved self-raising flour

25g cold butter, cut into small cubes

75g Cheddar cheese (mature), grated

150ml milk (plus an extra 2 tbsp
for glazing)

1 tbsp tomato ketchup

½ tsp Worcestershire sauce
– keep it local!

½ tsp salt

– METHOD –

1. Heat oven to 180°C/160°C fan/gas mark 4. Line a baking sheet.

2. Grill or fry the bacon on both sides until crisp and allow to cool.

3. Sieve the flour and salt into a bowl, add the butter and then rub in to make fine breadcrumbs.

4. Cut the crispy bacon into small pieces. Add to the bowl with one third of the cheese.

5. In a separate jug or small bowl, mix the milk, ketchup and Worcestershire sauce together. Pour into the flour mixture and stir to make a dough.

6. On a floured surface, shape the dough into an 18cm disc, brush with the remaining milk and cut into 8 wedges.

7. Place the wedges on the lined baking sheet and sprinkle over the remaining cheese.

8. Bake in the oven for 20–30 minutes until risen and golden brown.

· Breakfast In The · Early 1900s

As there were no fridges, food in the early 1900s had to be freshly prepared and cooked on a solid-fuel range. This meant there wasn't a huge variety of meals to choose from – unless of course you were very wealthy. Breakfast was one of the meals that tended to be the same every day. Eggs, bacon and bread were staple breakfast fodder – not much has changed in the last 100 years then!

Eggs Benedict

Story has it that in 1894, New Yorker broker Lemuel Benedict went to the Waldorf Hotel looking for a hangover cure and ordered toast, bacon, eggs and Hollandaise sauce. The hotel was so impressed, he put it on the menu. Gangsters in Birmingham had a strong connection with their counterparts in New York and Chicago – so if you find the fictional Luca Changretta at your breakfast table, whip him up this famous New York breakfast.

– INGREDIENTS –
Serves 4

225g butter, melted

¼ tsp salt

8 eggs

1 tsp vinegar

8 rashers of bacon

4 English muffins

2 tbsp butter, softened

Chopped fresh chives to garnish

For the Hollandaise sauce:

200ml white wine vinegar

200ml melted and skimmed unsalted butter

3 large egg yolks

1 tbsp peppercorns

1 tbsp lemon juice

– METHOD –

1. Boil the vinegar together with peppercorns and reduce the volume by half. Strain and reserve.

2. Boil a large pan of water, then reduce to a simmer. Using a large balloon whisk, beat together the yolks and the reduced wine vinegar in a heatproof bowl that fits snugly over the pan.

3. Beat vigorously, non-stop, until the mixture forms a foam – making sure that it doesn't get too hot. To prevent the sauce from overheating, take it on and off the heat while you whisk, scraping around the sides with a plastic spatula.

4. Gently whisk in the warmed butter, a little at a time, then return the bowl over a gentle heat to cook a little more.

· The Five Points Gang ·

Around the same time as the Blinders were at their peak, there were fearsome gangs aplenty in New York. Led by the Italian gangster Paul Kelly, the Five Points gang emerged in the 1890s and at one point had an incredible 1,500 members. They ran widespread racketeering and prostitution rings, along with robberies and generally fighting bloody turf wars with other gangs. It was the Five Pointers who introduced infamous gangsters Al Capone and Lucky Luciano to a life of organised crime and thuggery.

Remove from the heat again and whisk in another ladle of butter. Repeat until all the butter is incorporated and you have a texture as thick as mayonnaise. Finally, whisk in lemon juice, salt and pepper to taste. Put a lid on the bowl to keep the sauce warm.

5. Bring a large saucepan of water to the boil and then reduce to a simmer and add the vinegar. Very carefully break the eggs into the water and cook for around 3 minutes – the yolks should be soft in the centre. Remove the eggs from the water and put on a warm plate.

6. Fry or grill the bacon until cooked through. Split the muffins and toast them.

7. Butter the muffins and top each with a rasher of bacon and an egg. Drizzle with the sauce and then sprinkle on the chopped chives. Serve immediately.

· A Little Something Extra? ·

A breakfast after the night before might need a gentle dose of hair of the dog. But only if you're feeling a bit peaky of course! Beware of reinstating your drunken state. These cocktails are intended to perk you up, not set you on the road to ruin again.

Bloody Mary

This cocktail is an excellent hangover cure if you've had one too many at The Garrison. The origin of the Bloody Mary is unclear. Most of the theories point to its creation in the 1920s, but the definitive how and who created it are up for debate. Serve in a highball or pint glass.

Ingredients

45ml vodka
20ml lemon juice
Dash Tabasco sauce
5–10ml of Worcestershire sauce
Salt
Tomato juice
Stick celery
Slice lemon
Pepper (to taste)

Method

1. Fill the glass with ice. Add the vodka, lemon juice, Tabasco sauce, Worcestershire sauce and salt.

2. Top up with tomato juice and stir gently to combine.

3. Garnish with a stick of celery, a slice of lemon and grind some pepper on the top.

Mimosa

The Mimosa's sweet, citrusy orange juice combines with the bubbles of champagne to quench your thirst and boost your vitamin C. You'll soon be back on track and ready to start roaming the streets again. Serve in a champagne flute.

Ingredients

75ml orange juice
75ml champagne (or sparkling wine if your horse hasn't come in this week)

Method

Pour the orange juice into the glass and top up with the champagne. Garnish with a twist of orange peel.

Black Pudding Potato Cakes

Blood sausages. Not to everyone's taste but certainly bloody enough for the blinders! Especially associated with the Black Country and the West Midlands in England, hearty black pudding is thought to be the oldest form of sausage and was the perfect way to make sure that all the bits and pieces of a pig were put to good use and not wasted.

– INGREDIENTS –
Serves 4

800g cooked potatoes

50g butter

1 onion, sliced finely

2 garlic cloves, crushed

200g black pudding, cut into small cubes

100g mature Cheddar cheese, grated

2 tbsp rapeseed oil

4 fried eggs, to serve

– METHOD –

1. Preheat oven to 180°C/160°C fan/gas mark 4. Peel the potatoes and then grate them and pat dry.

2. Melt the butter in a large ovenproof pan. Add the onion, garlic and black pudding and cook until the onion is starting to soften. Remove from the heat and mix in with the grated potatoes and cheese. Season with salt and pepper.

3. Use your hands to shape the mixture into four potato cakes. Chill the cakes in the fridge for 30 minutes.

4. Heat the oil in a large frying pan and then fry the potato cakes for 2–3 minutes on each side or until lightly browned. Then transfer to the oven and bake for 15 minutes.

5. Serve topped with a fried egg. Cracking.

• Only In England •

Held on the Yorkshire/Lancashire border, the World Black Pudding Throwing Championship involves hurling a black pudding at a pile of Yorkshire puddings to see who can knock the most puddings over. The tradition is said to date from the War of the Roses in the 15th century when a group of soldiers ran out of ammunition and resorted to throwing black puddings at the enemy. Who needs a razor in their cap when they've got a sausage?!

Kedgeree To Die For

This traditional breakfast/brunch dish isn't exclusive to the Midlands, or even Britain, and traces its origins to India. Around the time of the Peaky Blinders, kedgeree had become a staple of British cuisine and featured in many recipe books in the late Victorian era – indeed, Queen Victoria was said to have been a big fan. For most, it was seen as a thrifty dish that could be made with inexpensive fish or leftovers.

– INGREDIENTS –
Serves 2

400g Basmati rice

2 eggs

120g smoked white fish
(usually smoked haddock but your choice!)

1 bay leaf

2–4 tbsp milk

1 tbsp butter

1 tbsp fresh parsley, chopped

1 tsp curry powder

4 spring onions, sliced

60g frozen peas

Salt and pepper to taste

NB: Don't be afraid to experiment with ingredients and make the most of your leftovers!

– METHOD –

1. Cook and drain the rice and allow to cool.

2. In a saucepan, cook the eggs in boiling water for 10 minutes until hardboiled. Remove from the heat and put them in cold water so they don't continue cooking. When cool, peel and chop into chunks.

3. Place the fish in a small pan with the bay leaf and add milk until the fish is just covered. Simmer gently until the fish starts to flake. Remove the fish and flake with a fork.

4. Melt the butter in a pan, stir in the curry powder, peas and spring onions. Fry for 2–3 minutes. Add the cooked rice, eggs, fish and parsley and heat all the ingredients through. Season with salt and pepper.

5. Serve the kedgeree hot or cold. Raise a glass to Queen Victoria.

· Cuts And Bruises ·

If you have an accident in the kitchen (or indeed if you encounter a gangster in a dark alleyway on your way home from The Garrison), try these old Black Country remedies to ease the pain:

Deep cut? Wrap it in a spider's web or apply the mould from the top of a jar of jam. Slightly more boringly, honey applied to a cut can assist healing.

Bruised? Break a leaf of houseleek (a succulent also known as *sempervivum*) in two and rub it on the bruise.

Tomato Dips

This simple dish is perfect for breakfast or brunch (and even as a starter for a traditional Black Country menu – see page 24). Cheap, cheerful and probably one of your five-a-day so a pretty good start to the day. However, if you want to make it a bit more traditional (and a lot less healthy!) replace the toast with bread fried in lard, dip the toast in the tomato mixture and then fry it again!

– INGREDIENTS –
Serves 2

120ml milk

4 large tomatoes, diced
(or 400g tin of chopped tomatoes)

½ small onion, chopped'

4 eggs, beaten

4 tbsp grated cheese

2 red chillies, finely chopped (optional)

Dash of Worcestershire sauce (optional)

Pinch of salt

– METHOD –

1. In a saucepan, simmer the onions, tomatoes and milk (plus any optional ingredients) until soft. Season.

2. Add the cheese and eggs and stir until the eggs are cooked.

3. Serve on thick, crusty, buttered toast.

· Did You Know? ·

The Black Country and Birmingham have suddenly been thrown into the limelight thanks to the *Peaky Blinders* TV show, but did you know that these famous names also hail from the region?

Lenny Henry, actor and comedian.

Beverley Knight, singer.

Julie Walters, actor.

Noddy Holder, lead singer of Slade.

Robert Plant, singer.

Black Sabbath frontman, Ozzy Osbourne, is also from Birmingham. In fact, actor Helen McCrory studied Ozzy's accent in order to prepare for her role as Polly Gray in *Peaky Blinders*.

How To Throw An Edwardian Dinner Party

The Peaky Blinders and their rival gangs spanned the later reign of Queen Victoria (1837–1901) and that of King Edward VII (1901–1910). Both momentous periods – one covering the industrial revolution and the latter the lead up to the First World War.

The Edwardian period was known for its elegance and luxury. In contrast, the preceding Victorian age was characterised by sweeping progress, political reform and social change. Despite this progress, in Edwardian times there was a huge difference between what the rich and poor ate. The rich lavished a lot of money on food; whilst the poor often had barely enough for one meal a day.

So, what do you need to throw a lavish Edwardian dinner party that will have your social circle talking for months?

– SERVANTS –

Not just an average servant – they need to be immaculately dressed, polite and extremely competent. If they let you down, they let down your good name and reputation! And be prepared to come down on them hard if they break one of your precious plates.

– REALLY PUSH THE – BOAT OUT

A top-notch Edwardian dinner party should have 8–10 courses. Yes, EIGHT to TEN. And each course should be as elaborate as possible to assure you of your reputation amongst your circle. You'll need an excellent chef – you'll have to pay them extremely well and put up with their tendency to be temperamental. But whatever it takes to impress …

– OOH LÀ LÀ! –

It was around this time that French cuisine became popular amongst the upper classes in Britain, helped along by King Edward VII's passion for continental luxury. If you want to make a statement of your sophistication, you will need to serve up some of the finest French delicacies – for example, beautiful patisseries, game and truffles – ideally washed down with champagne.

– AND DON'T BREAK – THE RULES ...

You might serve up the most delicious, exquisite meal, but if you don't watch your manners (or if you have a fork out of place) you will ruin the whole effect. For the Edwardians, there was a strict etiquette that covered everything from how the table was laid to the order in which courses were to be eaten.

In order not to bring shame on yourself and your family, familiarise yourself with the rules by perusing a book such as *Etiquette: Rules & Usages of the Best Society* (1886). Amongst the many rules needed to negotiate the minefield that is dinner, you'll learn that ...

• Greediness should not be indulged in.

• Indecision must be avoided. Do not take up one piece and lay it down in favour of another, or hesitate.

• Never allow a servant to fill your glass with wine that you do not wish to drink.

• Never use a napkin in place of a handkerchief.

Smokin' Starters

Black Pudding With Baked Roobub

The mighty black pudding coupled with sour rhubarb. Blood and flesh – what more could a Greedy Blinder want! Just don't let on that you're sweetening the roobub with sugar or you'll be thrown out the gang.

– INGREDIENTS –
Serves 4

110g rhubarb, ideally with thin pink stalks, cut into 2.5cm pieces

1 tsp white sugar

Freshly ground black pepper

50ml apple juice

1 tsp brown sugar

Salt

225g black pudding (cut into thick slices)

Olive oil

– METHOD –

1. Preheat the oven to 190°C/170°C fan/ gas mark 5. Put the rhubarb on a baking tray and sprinkle it with the sugar and some pepper. Cook in the oven for 10–15 minutes until soft (this will depend on the thickness of the rhubarb).

2. Leave the rhubarb to cook on the tray but transfer six chunks to a small pan to make the sauce. Add the apple juice, brown sugar and a pinch of salt to the rhubarb in the pan, bring to the boil and then simmer until it forms a syrup. Strain the syrup through a sieve.

3. Fry the black pudding in the olive oil until crisp on the outside.

4. To serve, place a slice of black pudding on the plate, top with the baked rhubarb and drizzle with the syrup.

· Lock Up Your · Kitchen Utensils

The real Peaky Blinders used inexpensive weapons – another reason it was unlikely they used razors, an expensive, luxury item at the time. Pretty much anything that came to hand was useful: from bricks to knives and steel toe capped boots. They could probably find a gruesome use for an icing bag if they needed to! However, their favourite weapon was a belt. Wrapped round a hand, thick belts with chunky buckles could cause horrible injuries when swung at the unfortunate victim.

Roasted Oysters With White Wine

If you don't want your starter preparations to be as complicated as a gangster's explanation of their business operations, try this simple appetiser. Back in the 19th century, oysters were plentiful and cheap – you might be impressing your modern-day guests but don't expect a Blinder to bat an eyelid!

– INGREDIENTS –
Serves 4–6

12 unshucked oysters

Coarse salt

White wine

– METHOD –

1. Preheat oven to 240°C/220°C fan/gas mark 9.

2. Spread a bed of coarse salt in a roasting pan. Lay the oysters on the bed of salt and bake until their shells start to open – around 5–10 minutes. Throw away any oysters that don't open – they're bad'uns!

3. Gently remove the top shells, being careful not to let any of the juice spill out. Then clip the lower muscles to release the flesh of the oyster.

4. Spoon 1 tbsp of white wine over each oyster, serve and enjoy.

• Common As Muck •

In the 19th century, oysters were very popular with the lower classes who used them as a cheap substitute for expensive beef in stews and soups. One of the most popular Victorian dishes was oyster pie. In 1864, over 700 million oysters were consumed in London alone. Hard to believe, especially when nowadays we associate oysters with champagne and the high life!

Lamb Croquettes

Croquettes grew in popularity in the 19th century and, if you were on a tight budget, were particularly useful as a way to reduce food wastage. You might like to save all your meat scraps from a week's worth of dinners to make these delicious crunchy fingers – or you could just buy some lovely lamb!

– INGREDIENTS –
Makes 12

500g leftover cooked potatoes

250g finely chopped or minced cooked lamb

25g Parmesan cheese, grated

2 tbsp flat-leaf parsley, chopped

100g plain flour

2 eggs

150g breadcrumbs

– METHOD –

1. Preheat oven to 200°C/180°C fan/ gas mark 6. In a large bowl, mash the leftover potatoes with a fork until smooth. Mix in the chopped cooked lamb. Add the Parmesan and flat-leaf parsley and season with salt and pepper. Use your hands to combine the ingredients thoroughly.

2. Divide the mixture into 12 and roll into log-shaped croquettes. Coat each croquette in flour, shaking off any excess.

3. In a bowl, beat the eggs with a fork and season with salt and pepper. Add the breadcrumbs to a separate bowl. Dip each croquette into the egg mixture and then into the breadcrumbs, coating well.

4. Heat 2–3 tbsp of vegetable oil in a frying pan over a medium to high heat. Cook the croquettes for 6–8 minutes, turning frequently, until all sides are golden. Place on a baking tray and then bake in the oven for 12 minutes.

5. Serve alongside a bowl of mint sauce for dipping.

· How To Keep A Husband ·

"… winning a husband is only a pleasure to a woman, but keeping him is a penance …. Conscious of her abilities and inabilities as a wife, a wise woman will learn how to keep a husband just as she learns how to keep house, to make chicken croquettes … and if she doesn't, why some syren [sic], with the sunshine in her tresses and the perfume of wild olives about her will secure for her a permanent vacation."

The Bismarck Daily Tribune, 1888

Sicilian Fish Soup

In the 19th century, the number of Italians emigrating to England grew steadily as rural life in Italy became a struggle. In the second half of the century, an Italian quarter known as Little Italy had established itself in Birmingham. Along with the cuisine they brought with them – like this incredible soup – came new rivals for gangs in London and Birmingham … the Sabini Gang.

– INGREDIENTS –

Serves 6

2 tbsp olive oil

1 onion

3 garlic cloves, chopped

18 green olives, minced

2 x 400g tins chopped tomatoes

700ml fish stock

15g fresh flat-leaf parsley, chopped

2 tbsp drained capers

¼ tsp dried crushed red pepper

900g fish fillets *(whatever type of fish you fancy!)*, cut into pieces

Salt and pepper

– METHOD –

1. In a large saucepan, heat the oil over a medium heat and sauté the onion for 5 minutes or until softened. Add the garlic and sauté for another minute. Add the olives, tomatoes, stock, parsley, capers and crushed red pepper and bring to the boil. Partially cover, reduce the heat and simmer for 10 minutes.

2. Add the fish to the pan, cover and simmer for around 10 minutes or until fish is opaque and flakes with a fork. Season with salt and pepper.

3. Serve with garlic bread.

· King Of The · Racecourse Gangs

Several of the characters in the *Peaky Blinders* TV show are based on real people. One such character is Charles 'Darby' Sabini, a powerful British Italian gang leader from London who ran horse racing extortion rackets. London gangs had a vicious war with gangs from Birmingham who were trying to control the same racecourses. A precarious truce was finally reached, with control of the racecourses split. After his empire fell apart, Sabini eventually ended up as a bookmaker in the English coastal town of Brighton – and a legitimate bookie at that. Quite a come down.

How To Throw A Black Country Dinner Party

You don't have to party like the Edwardian upper classes to enjoy an evening of fine snap! According to Pat Purcell's *Bostin' Fittle* (1978), this is the perfect plan for a traditional Black Country dinner menu …

Restaurant
MENU

First course

Tomato toast (see recipe for Tomato Dips on page 16) or a portion of Grey Peas and Bacon (see page 40).

Second course

Anything meaty! Try Oxtail Stew (see page 45) served with potatoes and fresh, seasonal vegetables. According to Pat Purcell:

"Amongst their many talents Black Country folk were adept at poaching and pheasant or rabbit were sometimes obtained …"
For authenticity it is not necessary to go poaching as bought ones taste nearly as good!

Third course — better known as pudding!

Bally Filler (page 70) and Jam Roly-Poly (page 71) are perfect to round up a meal in proper Black Country style. Follow with coffee and Whiskey Scuffles (page 79).

Main Dishes

Sides-salads

Drinks

Desserts

Smoked Salmon And Pickled Cucumber

The first freezers didn't appear until the 1940s and didn't go into mass production until after the Second World War. In the early 1900s, preserving food to feed your hoodlums was therefore not as easy as it is today. Pickling provided the perfect solution. This refreshing starter is the perfect combination of a showy luxury with a quick pickled veg.

– INGREDIENTS –
Serves 4

½ cucumber

1 tbsp white wine vinegar

1 tbsp lemon juice

Pinch of sugar

4 slices smoked salmon

1 little gem lettuce

– METHOD –

1. Separate the lettuce leaves, wash and set aside.

2. Using a vegetable peeler, peel the cucumber. Cut in half then scoop out the seeds, before slicing into fine strips.

3. Mix together the vinegar, lemon juice and sugar. When the sugar has dissolved, add the strips of cucumber and leave to stand for at least 30 mins.

4. Arrange 2–3 lettuce leaves per plate and place the smoked salmon on top. Finally, top with the pickled cucumber and serve immediately. Try adding caraway seeds or fresh ginger to the pickling mixture for additional flavour.

• Did You Know? •

Actor Cillian Murphy, who plays Thomas Shelby in Peaky Blinders, gave up 15 years of vegetarianism when he took on the role. He needed to bulk up to play Shelby, so his personal trainer suggested getting back on the meat wagon. In the meat and tripe-filled culinary landscape of the Peaky Blinder era, a vegetarian diet is near-impossible to imagine. Unless you were a rabbit of course. But then you'd have ended up in a pie.

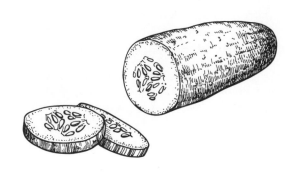

Devilish Devilled Eggs

Whilst not exclusive to England, these little devils were hugely popular in Edwardian times and no self-respecting plate of appetisers would be seen without them. The term to 'devil' a food means to cook it with spicy seasoning or over a very high heat. 'Stuffed eggs' is a much less fancy way to describe this dish, but the Shelby family would undoubtedly prefer the more devilish name.

– INGREDIENTS –
Serves 4

6 large eggs

3 tbsp mayonnaise

1 tsp Dijon mustard

1 tsp apple cider vinegar

Salt and pepper

Paprika

– METHOD –

1. Gently add the eggs to a saucepan of boiling water. Boil for 12 minutes, then remove from the heat, drain and put the eggs in a bowl of cold water.

2. When the eggs have completely cooled, peel them and slice in half lengthways. Remove the yolks carefully and set them aside in a bowl.

3. In the bowl, use a fork to mash the egg yolks. Stir in the mayonnaise, mustard, vinegar and salt and pepper.

4. Use a teaspoon to spoon the mixture into the hole in each of the egg whites. Sprinkle with paprika.

5. Serve with lettuce or any other salad green, for example rocket.

· Tales Of The Unexpected ·

Here are some old superstitions you might encounter in Birmingham and the Black Country …

If your child had a cough or a cold, feeding them fried or roasted mice was said to be an excellent cure!

Bread should be kneaded by hand to prevent pockets of air forming – these holes, called 'coffins', were said to be omens of death.

Use a knife (but take care not to use the point or cutting edge!) to mark your loaf of bread with a cross to protect it from witches. But don't use a fork as that's unlucky!

Dastardly Devilled Kidneys

Continuing the devilish theme from the previous recipe, devilled kidneys were originally a breakfast dish enjoyed by the Victorians and Edwardians but have also appeared in recipe books as a starter or supper. Kidneys and liver were seen as high in nutritional value and children were therefore encouraged to eat them. Even in those days, they were something kids tended to turn up their noses at!

– INGREDIENTS –
Serves 4

8 lamb kidneys, central membrane removed

1 tbsp Worcestershire sauce

1 tbsp lemon juice

2 tsp tomato purée or ketchup

1 tbsp English mustard

¼ tsp cayenne pepper

2 tbsp butter (unsalted)

1 tbsp parsley, chopped

1 tbsp spring onions, chopped

Salt and pepper to taste

– METHOD –

1. If the kidneys aren't already prepared, peel off the outer membrane then cut them in half and snip out the white core.

2. In a small bowl, whisk together the Worcestershire sauce, lemon, tomato purée or ketchup, mustard, cayenne pepper and salt and pepper.

3. Melt the butter in a frying pan over high heat, add the kidneys and fry for 2–3 minutes on each side.

4. Reduce the heat, add the sauce and stir until the kidneys are coated.

5. Serve on buttered toast and sprinkled with the spring onions.

• The Food Capital Of Britain •

Birmingham has been described as the 'food capital of Britain' thanks to its rich foodie history, melting pot of ethnic cuisines and array of fantastic restaurants. It is also the source of some of the nation's favourite brands, such as Bird's Custard, HP Sauce, Cadbury Chocolate, Bournville Drinking Chocolate and Typhoo Tea. There are over 100 Balti houses in the city and five Michelin-starred restaurants (more than any UK city outside of London).

Vicious Vichyssoise Soup

You'd be forgiven for thinking that this is a soup from France, but some believe that it was actually invented by a French chef at the Ritz-Carlton Hotel in New York in 1917. Whatever its origins, this creamy, luxurious soup, traditionally served cold, was a firm favourite in the early 1900s. French elegance or New York sass – either way, serve this and your sophistication will make you stand out from the gang.

– INGREDIENTS –
Serves 4

4 large leeks, sliced into rings

1 tbsp butter

1 onion, sliced

5 medium potatoes, peeled and sliced thinly

Salt and pepper, to taste

¼ tsp dried thyme

½ tsp dried marjoram

1 bay leaf

1l chicken stock

60ml whipping cream

– METHOD –

1. In a large saucepan or stock pot, gently melt the butter. Add the leeks and the onion and cook for 10 minutes, but do not allow to brown.

2. Add the potatoes to the pan and season with salt and pepper. Pop in the thyme, marjoram and the bay leaf, stir and then cover and cook for a further 12 minutes.

3. Add the stock, bring to the boil, reduce the heat and then cook for 30 minutes, partially covered.

4. Blend the soup in a blender or a food processor and leave to cool completely.

5. Before serving, stir in the cream. Serve cold. (For something more 'Peaky' than a bowl, serve in whiskey or shot glasses.)

• Did You Know •

The Peaky Blinders weren't the only criminals to famously come out of the Midlands. Professor Plum *et al* were hot on their heels after the Second World War. The boardgame *Cluedo* was invented in Birmingham by Anthony Pratt between 1943 and 1945. He based the idea – originally called *Murder!* – on the murder-mystery parlour games he used to watch being played when he worked as a pianist in country homes. Pratt had a fascination with the criminal mind and was an avid reader of murder fiction. Worldwide, the game has sold over 100 million units.

Waldorf Salad

Created at the Waldorf Hotel in New York in 1893, this world-famous salad has become a timeless American classic. The Depression of 1893 was one of the worst periods of economic difficulty in the US, yet the Waldorf Hotel stood in its midst as a glittery show of money and class, gangsters and politicians eating side by side as violent strikes raged.

– INGREDIENTS –
Serves 4

2 green apples

4 tsp mayonnaise

Juice of 1 lemon

4 celery sticks

50g grapes

50g walnut pieces

1 romaine lettuce

– METHOD –

1. Core the apples and then dice. Slice the celery widthways and chop the lettuce. Add the apple, celery and lettuce to a bowl with the grapes.

2. Stir in the mayonnaise and the lemon juice and mix thoroughly.

3. In a pan, gently toast the walnut pieces, taking care not to let them burn.

4. Serve the salad with the toasted walnuts sprinkled on top. Accompany with crusty bread.

• Oscar Of The Waldorf •

Oscar Tschirky was *maître d'hôtel* from the Waldorf's opening in 1893 until his retirement in 1943. Originally from Switzerland, Tschirky is credited with creating several classic recipes that brought his name and the hotel to the attention of the world: Waldorf salad, Eggs Benedict and Thousand Island dressing. These recipes continue to be popular to this very day.

Whiskey And Fiery Chilli Prawns

Liquor and fire! Sound a bit like the smoky backstreets of Brum? In this recipe, if the whiskey catches alight, simply take the pan off the heat and the whiskey will burn itself out. No need to literally recreate the hell of the criminal underworld.

– INGREDIENTS –
Serves 4

2 limes, zested and juiced

90ml whiskey

180g soft light brown sugar

20 uncooked prawns, peeled

1 red chilli, finely chopped

1 tbsp vegetable oil

– METHOD –

1. Preheat the oven to 200°C/180°C fan/ gas mark 6. Over a medium heat, heat the juice of the two limes, whiskey and sugar in a saucepan, stirring until the sugar has dissolved. Then, increase the heat and boil for around 6 minutes until the mixture thickens and turns syrupy.

2. Stir in the finely grated zest of one of the limes. Remove the pan from the heat.

3. Place the prawns in an ovenproof dish and sprinkle over the chopped chilli. Brush the prawns with the oil and then with the syrupy glaze from the pan.

4. Bake in the oven for 10–15 minutes or until the prawns are cooked through. Brush with some more glaze (any leftover glaze can be set aside as a dip).

5. Leave to cool slightly before serving with chunky bread.

• Did You Know? •

Quite a lot was happening in the culinary world at the peak of the Blinders …

The digestive biscuit was invented in 1892 by Alexander Grant.

In 1891, the first electric oven went on sale in the US, followed by England in 1893.

The first refrigerator for use in the home was invented in 1913.

The pop up toaster was invented by Charles Strite in 1919.

Pig's Head Terrine

Stop! Don't turn the page! The thought of a pig's head (known as 'brawn' when cooked) may turn your stomach but be brave and rise to the challenge. It might be one step beyond pig's trotters (page 47), but you won't be disappointed with the delicious results. Set aside your squeamishness and grab an enormous stock pot (at least 10 litres)!

– INGREDIENTS –
Serves 8

To cook the head:

Half a pig's head (*you'll need to make a special request to a butcher for this*)

3 onions, quartered

4 cloves garlic

1 stick celery, roughly chopped

2 carrots, roughly chopped

10g salt

10 peppercorns

2 sprigs rosemary

5 sprigs thyme

3 bay leaves

1 sage leaf

For the terrine:

1 clove of garlic, finely chopped

2 shallots, finely chopped

3 sprigs thyme, chopped

Oil for frying

Salt and pepper to season

Meat from the pig head

– METHOD –

1. To cook the pig's head: Place all the ingredients in a huge pan. Top up with water so that the pig's head is covered. On a low heat, simmer for 4 hours. Once it's cooled slightly, remove the pig's head.

2. Next step is to roll up your sleeves and get the meat off the head. It should fall off quite easily. Pick all the meat out of the head, making sure you separate the fat from the meat. Chop the meat into small pieces and set aside.

3. To prepare the terrine: Fry the shallots and garlic on a low heat until they soften. Once they've cooled, add them to the meat with the thyme, season with salt and pepper and mix thoroughly.

4. Line a terrine dish with cling film and fill with the meat mixture. Press it down to make sure it's compacted as much as possible. Put the terrine in the fridge for at least 8 hours (or ideally overnight) until set.

5. Serve with toast and chutney.

Herring Melts On Toast

Herring has long been one of our cheapest and most versatile fish – hence its popularity amongst the working classes in the late 18th and early 19th century. 'Melts' are the roes of male herring and they're so rich and creamy they literally melt in your mouth. They're also good for you as they're full of vitamin D. What's not to love?!

– INGREDIENTS –
Serves 4

500g herring roe ('melts')

1–2 tsp cayenne pepper

50g flour

50g butter

Lemon juice

– METHOD –

1. Wash the melts and gently dry with kitchen roll.

2. Mix together the flour and cayenne pepper. Roll the melts in the mixture.

3. In a pan, fry the melts for 3–5 minutes on each side, taking care not to overcook them or they'll lose their softness.

4. Add some lemon juice to the pan and turn the melts to coat them.

5. Serve on hot buttered toast with watercress on the side.

• In The Kitchen •

The 19th century, especially in the US, saw a huge expansion in the number of kitchen utensils available to buy. Labour-saving devices became popular, such as potato peelers and salad spinners. There were even devices advertised that would wash your dishes for you. They were a far cry from the modern dishwasher – think more of a carousel turned by hand that magically cleaned your plates without you needing to touch them!

Copper utensils were widely used and helped feed the copper industry in cities like Birmingham. However, copper utensils reacted with acidic foods and started to fall out of favour when other metals became available. By the turn of the 20th century, kitchen utensils were commonly made of enamelled iron and steel, nickel, silver, tin and aluminium.

Dressing For A Dapper Dinner

The Peaky Blinders didn't need to dress for dinner – they were *always* dressed for dinner. To this day, a 'blinder' is still common Birmingham slang for someone well-dressed and dapper. Their quasi-uniform made the gang members instantly identifiable – a badge of pride and belonging and a sign to mere mortals not to mess with them!

– GENTS –

To get this look, you literally need to be suited and booted ...

• Suit •

Full-on three-piece is the only suit that will do. Keep the trousers narrow-legged or you can go full Peaky and opt for flamboyant bell bottoms; either way, the length should be on the cropped side – as if you've just had a growth spurt. Tweed, checks and textured fabrics are the order of the day, preferably brown, grey or blue. Add a pocket watch for a dash of natty gent.

• Shirt •

Only a crisp white penny collar shirt will do. (Add some stripes if you're feeling a bit more extravagant.) A penny collar is halfway between a grandad shirt and a traditional collar shirt. Smart with a dash of cool.

• Boots •

Leather boots – lace up and above the ankle – will ensure you're part of the gang. Black or dark brown. (The boot length will also help you feel less embarrassed by your half-mast trousers!)

• Hat •

The crowning glory. The cherry on the cake. A newsboy/bakerboy cap is the must-have item to finish off your 'peaky' look – and it will hide your hair if your undercut has gone horribly wrong.

– LADIES –

Victorian and Edwardian fashion was decidedly buttoned-up so let's Charleston straight into the 1920s. It was in this decade that women's fashion found its freedom and cut loose from the starch of the preceding years. Beautiful and badass at the same time.

• Dress •

Think flapper. Think drop waist (perfect if you're indulging in some of the bally-filling foods in this book). Knee length or ankle length, choose beads and sequins that shimmer and shine.

• Shawl •

Evening dresses in the 1920s were distinguished from day dresses by their lack of sleeves. Up the glamour and warmth levels with a sophisticated silk or faux fur shawl (which can also double up as handy wrap for making off with your host's family silver).

• Jewellery •

Garnish your look with Art Deco-inspired brooches, strands of pearls or round beads, wide gem-studded bracelets and necklaces with tasselled ends.

• Feather Headband •

Quintessentially 1920s, a headband or clip with a feather completes the look. Peacock feathers were popular in the early 1920s and reflected the greens, blues and golds that were the common Art Deco colours of the era. White egret feathers were also a favourite. Wear feathers with caution if you (or your host) own a cat!

Bostin'
Mains

Faggits An Pays

Okay, so faggots probably aren't top of your list for a delicious main course, but we couldn't not include this much-loved Brummie dish. And it's loved for a reason! So, turn your nose back down and gives peas (and faggots) a chance.

– INGREDIENTS –
Makes 8 faggots

110g fatty pork shoulder

110g pig's liver

250g fatty belly pork

110g bacon scraps

110g breadcrumbs

1 medium onion (finely chopped)

½ tsp mace

1 tsp allspice

2 tbsp parsley (chopped)

2 sage leaves (finely chopped)

1 small red chilli (finely chopped)

Salt and pepper to taste

Caul fat *(Ask the butcher! If you can't find caul, you can use thin rashers of bacon instead.)*

• Origins Of The • Humble Faggot

Faggots have been popular in the Black Country for more than a century. Some say that they were the original takeaway food, long before fish and chips. The word 'faggot' means 'a bundle' and they're just that – a bundle of minced off-cuts and offal, traditionally wrapped in caul (the thin membrane that surrounds the internal organs of animals like pigs, sheep and cows). Originally, faggots were developed as a thrifty way to use up all the bits of pig that would otherwise be wasted, perfect when you couldn't afford to discard anything.

– METHOD –

1. Preheat the oven to 170°C /150°C fan/ gas mark 3. Roughly chop the pork, liver and belly pork and mince using a hand mincer. (You can also pop the meat in a food processor but be careful not to over chop it and create a sloppy mush.)

2. In a large bowl, mix together the minced meat, breadcrumbs, onion, herbs and spices. Season with salt and pepper.

3. Divide the mixture into 8 balls. Wrap each ball in caul, making sure it overlaps so that none of the mixture escapes faster than a Blinder from Inspector Campbell's clutches.

4. Put the faggots on a baking sheet and bake in the oven for 50–60 minutes.

5. Serve with mashed potato, mushy peas and a thick, rich gravy.

Chitterlings

Also known as 'chitlins' or 'chicklings', this traditional Black Country dish continues the theme of 'waste not, want not'. Chitterlings are the cooked small intestines of a pig. They're a bit chewy and not to everyone's taste. Oh, and they smell pretty horrible when you cook them. That said, although their popularity in the Midlands has declined, they are much-loved in the US!

– INGREDIENTS –

1.8kg cleaned chitterlings

1 large onion, chopped

355ml white vinegar

A few tablespoons of ground pepper

60ml fresh lemon juice

2 cloves of fresh garlic or a few dashes of garlic powder

568ml chicken stock

Seasoning salt

A few dashes of soy sauce

– METHOD –

1. Chop up your cleaned chitterlings (see below for how to do this properly!).

2. Add all your ingredients to a large saucepan.

3. Bring to the boil for 10 minutes then reduce to a simmer for 3 hours until the chitterlings are tender.

4. Serve with salt, vinegar and mustard, along with bread, fried bacon, onions or swede.

• How To Clean • Your Chitlins

Not for the squeamish. Imagine you're cleaning up after a brutal illegal bareknuckle fight – one speck of mess left and you're potentially in trouble with the police – or you'll be pretty poorly at least. Due to the potential for bacteria, chitterlings need to be boiled in water for 5 minutes, rinsed thoroughly several times in cold water and cleaned to remove extra fat, undigested food and specks of faeces (well, they are intestines!). To be doubly sure, turn them inside out, and clean them again.

Pork Pie

The pork pie is the most English of all savoury pies. With its thick crust, the pie is a conveniently portable snack, but it's also wonderful served cold in the summer with a huge salad, English cheeses and fresh, chunky bread.

– INGREDIENTS –
Makes 6 small pies

For the jelly:

470ml pork or chicken stock

1 sachet of powdered gelatine

For the pastry:

150g unsalted butter

720g plain flour

180g lard

300ml boiling water

1 egg, whisked

¼ tsp salt

For the filling:

907g boneless pork ribs,
cut into 1cm cubes

227g pork belly or fat back,
cut into 1cm cubes

227g thick bacon, cut into 1cm pieces

1½ tsp salt

1 tsp cracked black pepper

3 garlic cloves, minced

3 tsp fresh thyme leaves, chopped

2 tsp fresh rosemary, chopped

2 tsp fresh sage, chopped

½ tsp freshly grated nutmeg

– METHOD –

1. To make the filling: Mix the pork, bacon and fat chunks with all the herbs and seasoning and set aside.

2. To make the dough: Melt the lard in the boiling water. Put the flour and salt in a large mixing bowl and mix in the butter. Pour in the dissolved lard and water. Combine until a dough forms. Knead the dough by hand until it stops being sticky.

3. Divide the dough into six and take a small part of each to use for the pastry lids. Roll the portions of dough and flatten them out. Use a mould (for example the bottom of a jam jar) to create the shape of the pie. Try to keep the thickness of the pastry even as you shape it around the mould. Put the pastry and moulds in the fridge and chill for an hour.

4. For the lids, shape the pastry into rounds the same diameter as the pies. Chill in the fridge.

5. Preheat the oven to 180°C/160°C fan/ gas mark 4. Carefully remove the chilled dough from the moulds. Fill with the pork mixture, packing the pie more closely at the bottom and more loosely towards the top.

6. Cover with the pastry lids and crimp to seal the lid and sides of the pie together. Brush the top and sides with the whisked egg. Use a knife to cut a small hole in the centre of each lid. Place on a baking tray and cook in the over for 1 hour.

7. To make the jelly: Heat the stock in a saucepan, simmer and stir in the gelatine. When the pies are cooked, carefully pour the jelly into the top holes until each is filled. When the pies have cooled, put them in the fridge and leave them overnight to set.

· Poor Pigs ·

Pork pies as we know them today came into being in the 18th century and were especially popular in and around the East Midlands town of Melton Mowbray. Weirdly, this was down to something that isn't an ingredient in pork pies – cheese. The region's dairy industry produced a lot of whey, which was perfect for feeding pigs. Pigs were livestock that anyone could keep, including those people living in poverty, as pigs were happy to eat scraps and waste food. Pork therefore came to play a key part in the rural economy and eventually made its way into these delicious pies.

Grey Peas And Bacon

Nothing sounds more delicious that GREY peas, right? A pop of bright pea green amongst the dark, smoke-smudged factories might have brought a bit of cheer into the Peaky Blinders' lives. Traditionally, the peas are 'maple peas' – these days used frequently for bait for carp fishing, but still very much available for human consumption! This casserole is a popular warming supper on Bonfire Night or as an accompaniment to faggots.

– INGREDIENTS –
Serves 4

500g dried grey peas

1 large onion, sliced

85g pearl barley

Salt and Pepper

455g diced bacon (smoked or unsmoked)

1 litre vegetable stock

– METHOD –

1. Soak the peas and barley overnight in cold water – enough to cover them.

2. Drain any remaining water from the peas and barley. In a large pan, add the peas and barley to the onion.

3. Brown the bacon, chop it and then add it to the pan with the peas, barley and onion.

4. Add the stock and season with salt and pepper to taste.

5. Cook slowly for 2 hours.

· Pearls And Silk ·

Whilst pearl barley was a cheap ingredient, the girlfriends of gang members in Birmingham had something more lavish in mind – real pearls. Just as their boyfriends had a distinct, immaculate style, the ladies upped the glamour stakes with their love of elegant pearl earrings and necklaces. They also loved to wear brightly coloured silk handkerchiefs around their necks. Pearls and silk were definitely a sign that this was a woman not to be messed with – unless you wanted a 'friendly' visit from her boyfriend.

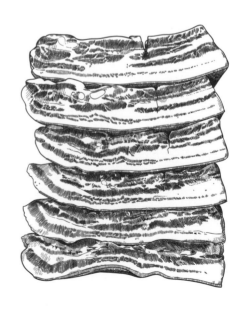

Boney Pie

Don't be put off by this unappetising name for what is actually a scrumptious meat pie! Bones from any animal (within reason!) can be used, but cheaply available pork bones were most commonly used in this traditional Black Country recipe.

– INGREDIENTS –
Serves 4

Bones and left-over cooked meat from your animal of choice

1 large onion, chopped

1 large carrot (*or any other root vegetables*), chopped

Salt and pepper, to taste

1 bay leaf

Herbs, fresh or dried
(*for example, marjoram, rosemary or parsley*)

Shortcrust pastry, ready-made

• Porky Pies •

No lie, Black Country butchers have a long history of producing delicious pork pies. Black Country families around Birmingham ate (and still eat) pork pie for breakfast on Christmas or Boxing Day. Before refrigerators were available, the pork pie crust served as edible Tupperware, allowing the meat to stay fresher for longer.

– METHOD –

1. Preheat oven to 220°C/200°C fan/gas mark 7.

2. In a large saucepan, cover the bones with water and bring to the boil. Simmer for 2–3 hours.

3. Spoon off any scum that rises to the top of the pan and then drain, setting the stock aside to use in the pie.

4. Heat a little oil in a pan and gently fry the onion and vegetables until soft.

5. Roll out the shortcrust pastry and line a deep pie dish. Add the bones and meat to the pie, along with the vegetables, bay leaf and herbs. Season to taste. Add some of the stock.

6. Cover the pie with a shortcrust pastry lid, prick, and bake for 25 minutes or until the pastry has browned. Serve with potatoes and fresh vegetables.

Lamb's Liver And Onions

A popular Black Country dish – and still enjoyed throughout England – lamb's liver is deliciously sweet, soft and quick and easy to cook. If you've not cooked liver before, don't panic – just remember not to overcook it or you'll lose its wonderfully soft texture.

– INGREDIENTS –
Serves 4

600g lamb's liver

2 tbsp plain flour

4 large onions, sliced

A few cloves of garlic, peeled and sliced

100g butter

500ml vegetable stock

2 tbsp plain flour

Salt and pepper, to taste

· Want To Be A · Peaky Blinder?

Thanks to the TV show, interest in the history of Birmingham and the Black Country had surged over the last few years. All kinds of real Peaky Blinder-inspired activities have sprung up, not only in their stomping ground but all over Britain and the world. You can attend themed parties and cruises, immersive experiences and escape rooms, eat Peaky Blinder burgers and drink Peaky Blinder spirits. A racket that the Shelby family surely wouldn't have missed out on! In fact, they'd probably be running all of it.

– METHOD –

1. Melt the butter in a pan, add salt and pepper and gently sauté the onions and garlic on a low heat for around 15 minutes or until they begin to caramelise.

2. Add the liver to the pan and fry gently until cooked through but not overdone. Remove the liver and set aside.

3. Stir the flour into the onion and garlic mixture and cook for one minute. Add the stock and heat until it thickens.

4. Serve the liver topped with the onion gravy, accompanied by mashed potatoes and peas.

Life For The Victorian Working Class

Queen Victoria's long reign lasted from 1837 to 1901. She would have seen a huge amount of change in her time as Britain transformed from a rural to an industrial society. Whilst the industrialists became rich as a result of trade and commerce, the workers lived, worked and died in very poor conditions.

– DOMESTIC CONDITIONS –

As a huge number of people moved to towns and cities to be near their workplace, there weren't enough houses to go around. Many people and families had to share rooms – sometimes 10 or more people in one room. Some factory owners built houses for their workers but these were usually cheaply and poorly built. The dirty streets and cramped living conditions were breeding grounds for disease. Rubbish was simply tossed into the narrow streets and the air was full of black smoke from the factory chimneys.

– WHAT DID THEY EAT? –

For poor Victorians, a typical breakfast usually consisted of bread smeared with dripping or lard (see page 61), with a bunch of watercress that provided vital vitamins and minerals.

Vegetables were cheap and seasonal veg was readily available in markets. Onions, cabbage, leeks, carrots and turnips were popular and perfect for the stews that were being simmered all over the country. For their fruit intake, people ate apples in winter and cherries in the summer. Thanks to street-corner vendors, the Victorians didn't want for healthy nuts, rich in fibre. Roasted chestnuts and cobnuts were often available on the street.

Meat was relatively expensive, so when people did buy it, they made sure that every last bit of it was used. No one could afford to waste anything. A good – and cheaper – alternative to meat was oily fish and seafood. Herrings, eels, oysters, cockles, whelks, cod and haddock were all popular.

Although the quantities of food might not have been huge, the diet available to the Victorian working classes was relatively healthy. Combined with all the exercise they got through manual and factory work, a fat working-class Victorian was very rare! It's also thought that Victorians suffered less from chronic diseases that we do. Coronary heart diseases and type 2 diabetes were relatively uncommon compared to now.

Contraband Chicken In Champagne

It's a wonderful show of opulence when you're so rich you can cook using champagne. (But don't worry if you can't afford champagne, any sparkling wine will do!) So, abandon yourself to the spirit of the Roarin' Twenties, imagine you're at a seedy jazz club and pop a cork to create this timeless classic.

– INGREDIENTS –
Serves 4

4 skinless and boneless chicken breasts

100ml lemon juice

60g butter

40g shallots, diced

2 medium garlic cloves, crushed

180ml chicken stock

180ml champagne

300ml double cream

1 tbsp olive oil

Salt and pepper, to taste

Handful of parsley, chopped

· Fizzy Pop ·

Queen Victoria is credited with making champagne popular in the UK. She insisted on serving it at all her banquets and society's wannabes of course followed suit! By the end of the 19th century, champagne had become part of popular culture. Advertising was promoting it as an aspirational product, associated with luxury and indulgence. It's no wonder that those with money – often of ill-gotten gains – were so proud to show off with a bottle of fizz.

– METHOD –

1. Sprinkle half of the lemon juice on the chicken breasts and season with salt and pepper.

2. In a pan, melt half the butter together with the olive oil. Brown the chicken for around 2 minutes on each side. When they are browned, remove the chicken from the pan.

3. Using the same pan, melt the rest of the butter and sauté the shallots until they're soft. Add the garlic and cook for another minute.

4. Add the stock, champagne (or cheaper sparkling alternative!) and the rest of the lemon juice. Bring to a boil and then simmer until reduced. Add the cream and cook over a medium heat for 5 minutes, or until thickened.

5. Add the chicken to the pan with the sauce and simmer until the chicken is cooked through completely (15-20 minutes).

6. Serve sprinkled with the chopped parsley, accompanied by pasta or rice.

Oxtail Stew

Long before oxtail became expensive, this old-fashioned cut was once a cheap choice for families when money was short. Rich and beefy, it's perfect for a luscious, warming stew on a winter's day. The only way to cook it is slowly!

– INGREDIENTS –
Serves 4

1.5kg oxtail

2 large onions, chopped

3 tbsp olive oil

1 can (400g) chopped tomatoes

4 medium carrots, peeled and chopped

2 large celery sticks, chopped

2 bay leaves

2 tsp dried rosemary

1 tsp dried thyme

1 litre beef stock

235ml red wine or water

2 tbsp plain flour

Salt and pepper, to taste

– METHOD –

1. Preheat the oven to 180°C/160°C fan/ gas mark 4.

2. In a large ovenproof casserole dish, heat 1 tbsp of olive oil and add the chopped onion. Cook for around 5 minutes until soft. Add the carrot and celery and cook for another 2–3 minutes. Remove from the heat.

3. In a large frying pan, heat the remaining olive oil and then add the oxtail. Cook until the oxtail is browned. Sprinkle the

• The Brummagem Boys •

Also known as the Birmingham Boys, these real-life criminals (who also featured in *Peaky Blinders*) were a powerful and violent street gang operating between the 1910s and 1930 and led by Billy Kimber. For several years, Kimber was the biggest organised crime boss in the UK. Interestingly, most of the Birmingham Boys came from London. They had a fearsome reputation and were said to kill rats by biting them. Perhaps that's where fellow Brummie Ozzy Osbourne got the idea for biting the head off a bat!

flour over the oxtail and stir to coat. Pour in the wine/water and stock, add the bay leaves, thyme and rosemary. Simmer for 5 minutes.

4. Add the oxtail and juices to the casserole dish with the onions, carrots and celery. Also add the chopped tomatoes. Bring to the boil and then remove from the heat and cover with a lid.

5. Place the casserole dish in the oven cook for 2 ½ hours or until the meat is tender and falls off the bone. If the gravy gets too dry during the cooking process, simply add water.

6. Serve with creamy mashed potato.

Pasta With Whiskey, Wine And Mushrooms

This definitely isn't a traditional West Midlands recipe. Nor is it likely to have appeared on the Shelby family dinner table. However, consider it a nod to the rivalry between the Peaky Blinders and the Sabinis – a smoky mix of whiskey and dry Italian wine to make your taste buds explode.

– INGREDIENTS –
Serves 4

340g portobello mushrooms, thickly sliced

2 tbsp olive oil

1 tbsp butter

1 medium onion, sliced

120ml dry white wine (Italian!)

120ml whiskey (Irish!)

60ml chicken stock

120ml double cream

Salt and pepper, to taste

340g pasta

– METHOD –

1. Preheat the oven to 190°C/170°C fan/ gas mark 5.

2. Drizzle the mushrooms with olive oil and season generously with salt and pepper. Roast in the oven for 25 minutes or until golden brown. Set aside.

3. In a large pan, heat the remaining olive oil with the butter over medium heat. Add the onions and sauté until they start to soften.

4. Add the wine and whiskey and allow to bubble for 1 minute. Pour in the stock and continue to cook until the liquid starts to reduce. Turn down to a low heat and stir in the cream. Add the mushrooms and season to taste. Simmer until the sauce thickens.

5. Serve tossed with pasta. This recipe is also delicious with cooked chicken.

· Fowl Play ·

Chicken wasn't the only bird enjoyed in Black Country cuisine. Along with the more conventional duck, goose and pigeon, rooks were sometimes cooked in pies. Only the breast was eaten as the rest of the bird was too bitter to consume. Getting a decent bird (or rabbit) for your family could well have marked the start of your criminal career – poaching was a huge problem, especially when times were hard and food was short.

Pig's Trotter Stew

In the past, there weren't many parts of a pig that we wouldn't happily eat. Ears, snout, tail … even the entire head boiled in a pot! Many of these we would probably pass over now – especially if we had to cook them ourselves. Pig's trotters were a traditional dish in the Black Country. If you can get over looking at them, you'll discover they're actually quite delicious.

– INGREDIENTS –
Serves 4

800g pork trotters, sliced
(and cleaned and prepared by a butcher)

1 onion, chopped

4 garlic cloves, crushed

2 bay leaves

1 litre chicken or vegetable stock

250g butternut squash, cubed
(or try carrots, parsnips or potatoes)

410g tinned brown lentils, drained

2 green chillies, chopped

Handful fresh parsley, chopped

1 tbsp vegetable oil

Salt and pepper, to taste

– METHOD –

1. Season the trotters with salt and pepper. Heat the vegetable oil in a large saucepan and cook the trotters until browned.

2. Add the onion, garlic, butternut squash and bay leaves and stir thoroughly. Pour in the stock and bring to the boil.

3. Cover and simmer for 3 hours, or until the trotters are tender and the meat is starting to come away from the bone. (If the stew becomes dry during cooking, just add water.)

4. Add the lentils, chillies and parsley and season with salt and pepper. Heat until the lentils are warmed through.

5. Serve with mashed potatoes and fresh vegetables.

· This Little Piggy · Went To Market

If you're looking to buy something more unusual like pig's trotters, a visit to a butcher or a market is your best bet. Transport yourself back in time to the late 1800s and early 19th century and you'd be able to visit the pig market in Birmingham, a far cry from modern-day meat markets. Commercial pig production was rare before 1900, so you may have bought your own pigs to keep in your backyard. In fact, this was encouraged during the First World War so that you'd have a guaranteed source of protein.

Sausage And Mash Bake

If you're in need of comfort food to feed the whole family then look no further. The only thing more comforting than sausages is sausages AND mash. Simple to prepare and cook, it'll look like you've put far more effort into it than you have. So, if you've had a rubbish day at the factory, or your latest consignment of illegal booze has disappeared somewhere in Birmingham's canal system, enjoy this meal and forget all your worries.

· Did You Know? ·

Thanks to the Romans, sausages have been enjoyed in Britain since before 400AD.

There are more than 500 recipes and flavours for sausages in Britain. Taking into account all the different variations across the country, you could probably eat a different British sausage every day for ten years!

English counties, towns and cities each have their own unique way of flavouring their local sausage. For example, Lincolnshire uses fresh sage, Cheshire uses caraway and coriander, a Manchester sausage includes ginger, sage, mace, nutmeg and cloves. In the Midlands, the tomato sausage is popular – the pork is mixed with tomato giving the sausage a sweet flavour and red/orange colour.

Sausages gained the nickname 'bangers' during the Second World War. During the war, ingredients were scarce so sausages had a high water content – this meant they were liable to explode during cooking when the water turned to steam!

– INGREDIENTS –
Serves 4

1kg floury white potatoes

8 sausages *(ideally something traditional like Cumberland)*

Bunch chives, chopped finely

Bunch spring onions, sliced widthways

2 onions, peeled and sliced

6 sprigs thyme

50g unsalted butter

50ml full fat milk

½ tbsp olive oil

1 tbsp balsamic vinegar

1 tbsp redcurrant jelly

100ml red wine

400ml chicken stock

2½ tsp cornflour

1 tbsp cold water

150g frozen peas

– METHOD –

1. Preheat the oven to 180°C/160°C fan/ gas mark 4.

2. Boil the potatoes until cooked then mash with the butter and milk. Stir in the chives and spring onions.

3. Heat the oil in a pan and fry the onion until it softens. Add the vinegar, redcurrant jelly and the wine and bring to the boil. Add the stock. Simmer for 3 minutes.

4. Mix the cornflour with the cold water to form a runny paste. Stir into the pan to create a thick gravy. Sprinkle with half of the thyme leaves.

5. Put the sausages in an ovenproof dish and pour over the gravy. Sprinkle with the peas and then top it all with the mash and a final sprinkling of thyme.

6. Bake in the oven for 25 minutes. Check the sausages are cooked through before serving.

7. Enjoy with green veggies – or some baked beans if you fancy full-on comfort!

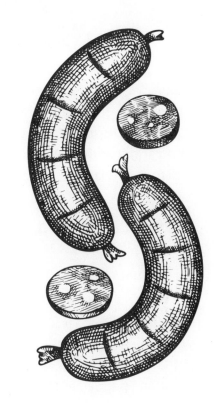

Snitchers' Bubble And Squeak

Offal, pig's trotters, bones ... we've seen how folk were adept at using up leftover meat and the 'forgotten cuts'. But how about using up vegetables? Bubble and squeak, of course! Whilst it might sound like something a snitch would do under interrogation by a gang boss, this dish is the best way to enjoy a stray sprout and a lonely carrot.

– INGREDIENTS –
Serves 2

15g unsalted butter

75g onion, chopped

450g cooked potatoes, mashed

150g leftover cooked veggies, chopped
(e.g. cabbage, sprouts, carrots, peas, parsnips)

Salt and pepper, to taste

– METHOD –

1. In a large frying pan, melt the butter over medium heat. Add the chopped onion and fry for around 3 minutes or until soft.

2. Mix together the mashed potatoes and vegetables and add to the pan. Increase the heat slightly and fry for 10 minutes. Turn the potatoes and vegetables so that they get heated through.

3. Press the mixture down into the pan to brown the edges and leave to cook for 1 minute. Turn the mixture and repeat on the other side.

4. Serve with cold, roasted meat (more leftovers!).

• The Brighton Razor Gangs •

Gang warfare was by no means limited to Birmingham and London. All over the country, people were struggling to get by and many youngsters would turn to crime for money and for kicks. The Brighton razor gangs were groups of razor-wielding youths embroiled in racketeering at the local racecourses (where else?!) in the 1930s and 40s. Amongst the gangs causing chaos in Brighton were the Sabini gang, real-life rivals of the Peaky Blinders.

The Rise Of Fish And Chips

There are few things more British than fish and chips. They're an institution. Debate rages over where in England this mouth-watering combo originated and it's unlikely anyone will ever agree! Regardless of where fish and chips came from, the mid-19th century saw the rapid rise of this classic meal across Britain.

– THE FIRST FISH AND – CHIP SHOP?

Lancashire lays claim to the first fish and chip shop, where Mr Lees was said to be serving them from a hut on the market in 1863. However, travel a couple of hundred miles south to London and you'll be told that Joseph Malin opened the first fish and chip shop in 1860.

– WHY WERE THEY – SO POPULAR?

Aside from being delicious and easy to cook, serve and eat, fish and chips were a cheap meal and fuelled hardworking ordinary folk. From the mid-19th and into the 20th century industrialism was booming and, as it rapidly grew, so did the number of workers who wanted to eat fish and chips. By 1910, there were 25,000 fish and chip shops across the UK. By 1930, there were more than 35,000!

– DID YOU KNOW? –

Fish and chips could be served in newspaper until the 1980s when it was decided that to have the food touching newspaper ink was unhealthy.

The oldest fish and chip shop still running is near Leeds in England. It is said that fish and chips have been served there continually since 1865.

During the World Wars, the government went to great lengths to avoid rationing fish and chips, fearing it would damage the public's morale if they did.

The most popular sauce to have with your chips in Birmingham is curry sauce.

The saying goes that you should never eat fish and chips where you can't see the sea. This isn't good news for the West Midlands and the stomping ground of the Peaky Blinders – it's landlocked!

In the UK, there are now around 10,500 fish and chip shops. Far less than there used to be, but the dish still remains one of the nation's ultimate comfort foods.

Fish And Black Country Orange Chips

Orange chips are considered a delicacy in the Black Country. Just why they are so delicious and how they originated is a bit of a mystery and you'll hear different stories from fish and chips shop owners. What makes these chips distinct is the way they're dipped in batter before they're deep fried. Sounds unhealthy? Yes. But sounds delicious? Absolutely!

– INGREDIENTS –
Serves 3–4

4 large potatoes

½ tsp salt

½ tsp black pepper

½ tsp garlic powder

½ tsp paprika

120g plain flour, plus to coat the potatoes

1 tsp baking powder

250ml milk

125ml water

A few drops of orange food colouring

Cooking oil for deep frying

– METHOD –

1. Peel the potatoes then cut into chip-sized chunks.

2. To make the batter, add the salt, pepper, garlic powder, paprika, flour and baking powder to a bowl and mix. Slowly add the milk and water, whisking until smooth. Add the food colouring and mix.

3. Coat the cut potatoes with flour and dip them in the batter.

4. Gradually add chips to a preheated deep fat fryer or large pan. Cook until golden on all sides. Remove from the pan and allow to cool slightly.

And now for the fish ...

– INGREDIENTS –
Serves 4

4 x 175g white fish fillets

Batter ingredients as per the recipe for orange chips

Cooking oil for deep frying

– METHOD –

1. Lightly coat the fish fillets in flour. Make up the batter mixture as in the recipe for chips.

2. Dip two of the fillets in the batter and gently lower into a preheated deep fat fryer or large pan. Fry for 6–7 minutes until crisp and golden orange. Drain on kitchen towel and keep warm whilst cooking the remaining two fillets.

3. Serve your fish and chips wrapped in yesterday's newspaper (or maybe not – see the note on health and safety on page 51!) – or a plate will do. Accompany with mushy peas or traditional Black Country Grey Peas (see page 40, minus the bacon).

· Best Black Country · Fish And Chip Shops

If you are ever in the area, here are some of the best fish and chip shops to visit, according to review site TripAdvisor (2020):

Bobbo's Today's Catch Restaurant and Takeaway

1-2 Long Lane, Rowley Regis, Sandwell B65 0HT

The Island House

160 Stafford Road, Oxley, Wolverhampton WV10 6JT

Miss Fish

1 Hagley Road, Halesowen B63 4PU

Ablewell Fish Bar

72 Ablewell St, Walsall WS1 2EU

Penn Chippy

329 Penn Road, Wolverhampton WV4 5QF

Carl's Fish and Chips

17 Ridding Lane, Wednesbury, Sandwell WS10 9AA

Aldridge Chippy

27 Anchor Road, Walsall WS9 8PT England

Oldswinford Fish and Chips

140 Hagley Road, Stourbridge DY8 2JD

Groaty Pudding

No book that includes Black Country recipes would be complete without groaty pudding. What's a groat? Well, for once it's not an unusual cut of meat! Groats are a cereal wholegrain, such as rye, barley, oat and wheat. This savoury pudding is amazing if you're in dire need of comfort food. In the Black Country, it's traditional to eat groaty pudding on Bonfire Night.

– INGREDIENTS –
Serves 4

400g chunks of beef stewing steak

2 onions, finely chopped

2 leeks, chopped

3 carrots, chopped

200g pearl barley

500ml beef stock

2 tbsp Worcestershire sauce

1 tsp dried rosemary

Salt and pepper to taste

2 tsp cornflour

– METHOD –

1. Preheat oven to 160°C/140°C fan/gas mark 3–4.

2. Put all the ingredients except the cornflour in an ovenproof dish with a lid. Stir to combine thoroughly.

3. Put a lid on the casserole dish and cook in the oven for 5–6 hours.

4. When cooked, the consistency of the pudding needs to be thick. If it needs thickening, add cornflour and water and put back into the oven until thick.

5. Serve with crusty bread and a contented smile, safe in the knowledge that a satisfied belly is on the cards.

• The First Peaky Blinder •

Henry Lightfoot (1873-1936) is thought to have been the first person to be referred to as a 'peaky blinder'. Lightfoot was a thug and criminal who lived in Garrison Lane in Birmingham. He had his first spell in prison in the early 1900s for assault and went on to become a member of Birmingham's notorious street gangs. Lightfoot was well known for his fights with the law and once took on the Hays Mill police single-handedly. Brave or stupid?

Soused Herrings

In 1872, the Cheapside Slogging gang (see page 61) rioted in Birmingham, smashing windows, stealing from shops and attacking store owners and terrorising locals who tried to intervene. Of the 400 or so gang members involved, only three arrests were made – one of which was for stealing herrings from the market hall. Let's hope the herrings stolen were beautifully cooked and marinated like in this recipe so they still tasted good when the young scallywag was released.

– INGREDIENTS –
Serves 6

6 fresh herrings (approx. 200g each)

1 sprig fresh thyme

2 bay leaves

2 tsp sea salt

1 large onion, thinly sliced

300ml water

300ml dry white wine

100ml white wine vinegar

6 black peppercorns

½ tsp mustard seeds

2 tsp brown sugar

– METHOD –

1. Preheat the oven to 180°C/160°C fan/ gas mark 4.

2. Scrape the scales off the herrings. Cut off their tails and heads. Remove the guts and clean them thoroughly, keeping the soft roes. Wash the herrings again under running water and then pat them dry. Put the roes back and then lay the herrings in a dish, placed heads to tails. Or ... ask a fishmonger to do it for you!

3. Cover with the water, vinegar and wine. Sprinkle on the salt, peppercorns and mustard seeds, then add the thyme and bay leaves. Finally, sprinkle with the brown sugar.

4. Cover with a sheet of foil and then stand the dish in a roasting tin of boiling water.

5. Bake for 30 minutes and then allow to cool.

6. Serve with buttered bread and salad.

• Herrings ... Did You Know? •

A whole herring that has been split from tail to head, gutted, salted or pickled, and then cold-smoked is a kipper.

A 'bloater' is a type of cold-smoked herring that was popular in the 19th century and early 20th century. Unlike kippers, they aren't gutted but are salted and smoked whole. Their name refers to how they swell when being prepared.

Beef Marrow With Oxtail Chutney

Humans have been eating and enjoying bone marrow since the year dot. It's even credited as contributing to the evolution of our brain power! Marrow is an underappreciated food these days but well worth a try. Flavour-wise, it has a subtle, creamy nuttiness and sweet richness. Plus, it's full of vitamins and minerals – in fact, beef tea used to be hugely popular across Britain as a way to use up bones and benefit from the nutritional goodness beef provided.

– INGREDIENTS –
Serves 6

For the beef marrow:

1.4kg centre-cut beef marrow with the bones cut into 5cm pieces and the tendons trimmed *(if you don't fancy doing this, your butcher will do it for you!)*

75g salt

For the chutney:

1.8kg oxtail, trimmed

1.4l port wine

1.4l dry red wine

3.8l chicken stock

1 bulb of garlic

½ bunch fresh thyme

1 tbsp black peppercorns

110g unsalted butter

25g plain flour

680g carrots, peeled, trimmed and cubed

450g shallots, peeled and cubed

½ tsp salt

100g granulated sugar

100g light brown sugar

236ml red wine vinegar

2½ tsp freshly ground black pepper

Fresh flat-leaf parsley leaves, to garnish

– METHOD –

1. Mix the salt with 950ml cold water and pour over the bones in a large bowl. Make sure the bones are covered. Place the bowl in the fridge for 36 to 48 hours or until the bones are bleached of colour. Change the water three times. Drain.

2. In a large stock pot, mix together the oxtail, half of the port wine, the red wine, stock, garlic (slice the bulb in half), thyme and peppercorns. Bring to the boil and then reduce the heat and simmer for 3 hours.

3. Next, when the oxtail is cool enough, transfer it to a bowl. Remove the meat from the bones and cut into small cubes. The oxtail can be popped in the fridge until you're ready to use it.

4. Strain the juices from the oxtail mixture into a large pan (no need to keep the solids). Bring to the boil and then simmer for around 2 hours, until the mixture is reduced.

5. While it reduces, in a separate small bowl, combine one third of the butter with the flour to form a paste. Gradually add the paste to the reduced liquid, stirring constantly until the liquid thickens.

6. In another pan, melt the rest of the butter. Add the carrots, shallots and a pinch of salt and sauté until softened. Stir in the granulated and brown sugar, the rest of the port, red wine vinegar, salt and 1½ tsp of the black pepper. Cook on a medium heat until the liquid has completely evaporated (around 45 minutes). Mix in the oxtail meat, thickened oxtail liquid and the rest of the black pepper. Set aside.

7. Arrange the bones on a serving platter. Spoon the oxtail chutney around the bones and then sprinkle with salt and the fresh chopped parsley. Serve with mashed potato and seasonal greens.

Blood Sausage With Beetroot, Apple And Fried Egg

There isn't an ingredient in this dish that's not to love. Earthy beetroot, the bloody tang of black pudding and the crispness of apple – all topped with a sumptuous fried egg. Did you know that in the mid 19th century, wine was often coloured with beetroot juice? The other use for beetroot juice at the time was as a cheek and lip stain for women – hence the saying 'red as a beet'.

– INGREDIENTS –
Serves 4

1 tbsp olive oil

500g blood sausages *(black pudding)*

2 tsp honey

2 tbsp apple cider vinegar

1 red apple, cut into matchsticks

1 beetroot, peeled and shredded

25g mint leaves

2 tbsp pine nuts, toasted

4 eggs, fried

Fresh parsley, chopped

– METHOD –

1. Heat the oil in a frying pan. Over a high heat, add the sausages and cook for 8–10 minutes or until cooked through, turning occasionally. Transfer the sausages to a plate and set aside, keeping them warm.

2. Put the frying pan back on the heat and add the honey and vinegar. Cook for 1 minute or until the mixture has reduced slightly. Remove from the heat.

3. Add the sausages to the pan along with the apple, beetroot, mint leaves and pine nuts. Gently combine all the ingredients.

4. Season and serve immediately, each serving topped with a fried egg and sprinkling of parsley.

• The Black Hand •

You're very likely to get red hands from cooking the above recipe thanks to the beetroot and black pudding. But, better to get a red hand than a black hand. In *Peaky Blinders*, the Shelby family started to receive Black Hands – should they have been worried? Yes! The Black Hand can be traced back to Naples in the 18th century, but by the early 1900s it was being used by Italian communities in the UK and US. It involved sending a letter to the victim, making threats in return for money. The letter would be decorated with threatening symbols – for example, a noose or gun – and signed with the inky black imprint of a hand. The practice gradually died out when criminals realised there were easier ways to extort money from people!

Sneaky Sides And Snacks

Aunt Polly's Pikelets

Pikelets are a popular snack in Brummie households. Quicker to make than a getaway, they're the perfect pick-me-up when you get home from a hard day masterminding a criminal gang. Don't confuse them with crumpets – pikelets are thinner and, because they contain no yeast, they're about as hol(e)y as one of Polly Gray's confessions.

– INGREDIENTS –
Makes around 14 pikelets

150g self-raising flour

1 tbsp caster sugar

185ml milk

1 tbsp white vinegar

1 egg

A little bit of melted butter

Pinch of salt

– METHOD –

1. Mix the flour and sugar together in a bowl with the pinch of salt.

2. Add the vinegar to the milk and let it thicken.

3. Whisk the milk/vinegar mixture and the egg together. Then add the melted butter and add to the bowl of dry ingredients, whisking until smooth.

4. Heat a non-stick frying pan over medium heat. Drop level tablespoonfuls of the mixture into the pan and cook for 30 seconds or until bubbles appear on the surface.

• Polly's Pikelet Etiquette •

Sass isn't in the ingredients list but, if you want to cook a pikelet like the fictional Polly Gray, you'll need it in bucketloads.

1. Ditch your apron for something more dramatic. Perhaps a 1920s silk and lace cocktail dress, finished off with a string of pearls and an ostrich feather in your hair.

2. It's okay to cry if you spill the milk. Polly may seem like she's made of steel but she has more emotional depth than the rest of the Shelbys put together.

3. If you have guests around for pikelets, they need to wait their turn. Family always comes first.

4. And, when you can't face another buttered pikelet, remember, as Polly says: 'Brave is going where no man has gone before'. Be adventurous with your toppings!

5. Turn and cook on the other side for 1 minute until golden.

6. Allow to cool and serve with butter, jam and cream. Or whatever you fancy!

Black Hand Bread And Dripping

If you're of a certain age, there's a very good chance you will have heard your parents or grandparents rave about the artery-blocking treat that is bread and dripping. This isn't something you should be snacking on daily if you want to live a long and healthy life, but well worth a try to see what all the fuss was about!

– INGREDIENTS –
(quite simple!)

Dripping

Bread

– METHOD –

Ideally, for the dripping, you should save the juices from a roasted joint of beef or pork and leave in a container to set. If that's not possible, you can make your dripping from scratch as follows:

1. Remove the surplus fat from some pork or beef. Alternatively, ask a butcher if you can buy some of their fat trimmings.

2. Slowly fry the pieces of fat in a pan. The fat should melt away as you cook it. Use a splatter guard to save your dapper garments from any hot splashes.

3. As you cook, transfer the hot, melted fat into a heatproof storage container. Continue cooking until most of the fat has turned to liquid. You can also add any crispy bits to your dripping mixture for extra flavour.

4. Leave to cool and then store in the fridge. The dripping will separate into two layers – a top fat layer and a lower jelly-like layer.

5. Serve on thick, crusty bread or toast. The combination of the two layers of dripping spread thinly (or thickly – but think of your waistline!) is to die for.

• The Slogging Gangs •

Before the Peaky Blinders started to wreak their own brand of havoc, the Slogging gangs were turning the working-class districts of Birmingham into no-go zones. Major slogging riots were commonplace between rival gangs such as the Ten Arches gang, the Nechells Sloggers and the Park Street gangs. Whilst they might sound like something straight out of the *Beano*, they were particularly nasty and their violence steadily grew worse. By 1895, the gangs were being referred to as 'Peaky Blinders'.

Pork Razor Scratchings

Pork scratchings are believed to have their origin in the Black Country in the 1800s. They were a food of the working classes, where families kept their own pigs at home, feeding them up for slaughter. Pig skin became yet another piece of the animal that was made good use of! They're now a hugely popular bar snack enjoyed everywhere.

– INGREDIENTS –

Serves 6–8 (but probably just you – VERY moreish!)

Rind from a leg of pork
(this should include a thin layer of the fat to help cook it)

Sea salt

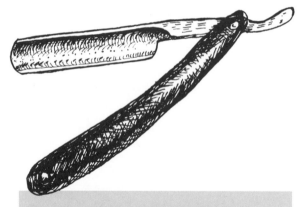

– METHOD –

1. Heat the oven to 200°C/180°C fan/gas mark 7.

2. Score lines widthways – about 1cm deep and 1cm wide – across the rind. Pat with kitchen paper to thoroughly dry the fat and rind.

3. Rub salt all over, including in the slits of the rind. Be generous with the salt!

4. Place on a baking tray and cook for 30 minutes or until crisp and golden. (If it snaps and breaks apart easily, it's done.)

• Hairy Moments •

Ask a child to draw a pig and they'll draw it pink, round and smooth. In fact, pigs are pretty hairy beasts and the last thing you want is to get a pig hair caught between your front teeth while you're enjoying your scratchings. Carefully check your pork rind before putting it in the oven. Be like a Peaky Blinder – never have a hair out of place.

Restaurants On The Up

Have you ever wondered where the concept of a restaurant as we know it today comes from? Well, you can thank an uprising that didn't involve any Peaky Blinders. After the French Revolution ended in 1799, thousands of chefs who had been working for aristocratic and royal households suddenly found themselves unemployed. They turned their culinary skills to providing citizens in the newly egalitarian society with sophisticated and well-cooked food. The French middle classes – enjoying their new-found power – started to turn dinnertime into a social experience and restaurant society was born. Until then, the concept of going out for a meal in public didn't exist.

Restaurants reached Britain in the 1880s. In England in the 18th century, there was an early evening dinner, between about 5–6pm. In Victorian times in the 19th century, with people out at work, this was moved to 8–9pm and became called 'supper'. Restaurants serving dinner only were known as 'supper rooms' and people sat communally at large tables. There would be a set menu with various courses, but you couldn't choose what you ate. (The idea of the *à la carte* menu wasn't introduced until 1899.)

The menu did not change from week to week (likewise there would be no 'specials' board). However, there was a different menu for each day of the week that repeated week on week, whatever the season. In many restaurants, Tuesdays, Thursdays and Saturdays were baking days, so if you were lucky there might be extra special treats on the menu.

A restaurant table setting in Victorian times was very complex. There were vases of flowers, candles, tablecloths, doilies, napkins and the best crockery and silverware that could be afforded. Glasses were for water and wine. Woe betide you if you didn't follow the appropriate etiquette!

By the Edwardian era, Britain was in a golden age of restaurants. Leading the way was King Edward VII with his love of luxury and decadence – Edwardians just never seemed to stop eating! Hotels began to remodel their dining rooms into fashionable restaurants, with terraced dining, winter gardens and separate supper rooms for private parties. An American influence also arrived with the introduction of the 'bar' and the 'grillroom', a room set aside for informal dining.

Cob Rolls

A cob is the local word for a crusty bread roll, supposedly because the small round loaves look like cobblestones. These go with anything and everything and are a perfect accompaniment to any of the soups and stews featured in this book. If you want a snack on the go, a cob roll will also fit neatly under your bakerboy cap!

– INGREDIENTS –
Makes 12 rolls

400g strong wholewheat or white flour

280ml warm water

7g sachet Easy Bake Dried Yeast

1 tsp salt

1 tbsp caster sugar

1 tbsp oil

– METHOD –

1. In a bowl, mix together the flour, yeast, salt and sugar. Add the water and oil and combine well.

2. Tip the mixture onto a lightly floured surface and knead for 10 minutes until smooth and stretchy.

3. Put the dough back in a bowl, cover and leave in a warm place for 1–2 hours, or until doubled in size.

4. Grease a baking tray with oil. Divide the dough into 12 pieces and shape each one into a ball. Put them on the baking tray, leaving plenty of space between them.

5. Cover the baking tray with clingfilm and leave for an hour.

6. Preheat the oven to 220°C/200°C fan/ gas mark 7.

7. When the rolls have doubled in size, uncover and sprinkle with flour. With a knife, make a cross on top of each roll.

8. Bake in the oven for 15 minutes or until golden brown. They should sound hollow when you tap them. Place on a wire rack and leave to cool.

• Alfie Solomons •
– fact or fiction?

In the TV programme *Peaky Blinders*, Alfie Solomons ran an illegal distillery under the guise of a bakery. The character is loosely based on a real-life Jewish gangster from the early 1900s. The real Alfie Solomon (minus the 's'), along with his brother Harry, worked with the Sabini gang to control racecourses around the country and to run protection rackets around Clerkenwell and Farringdon in London. Whilst not as powerful as the fictional Alfie Solomons, he was an important part of the operation. He was also arrested in connection with the shooting of Birmingham gangster Billy Kimber.

Peaky Puddings
And Sweet Stuff

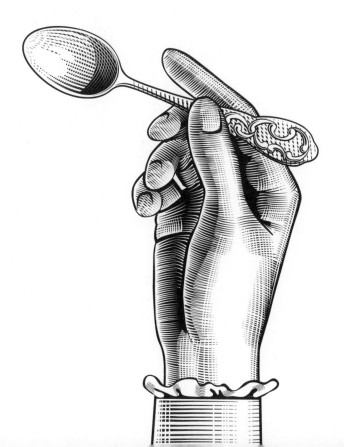

Syrupy Vanilla Rice Pudding

A wonderful pudding to enjoy on a cold winter's evening. Forget all memories of the rice pudding you were served at school. Whilst this recipe harks back to the good old days, you'll find it infinitely more delicious and creamy than the standard school version. Its sweetness will gently stroke your taste buds. And you won't even to have to ask Granny if you can lick the golden syrup off the spoon.

– INGREDIENTS –
Serves 6

500ml full fat milk

500ml double cream

50g caster sugar, plus extra for sprinkling

180g pudding rice

1 vanilla pod, split lengthways
and seeds scraped out

Golden syrup, to serve

– METHOD –

1. In a pan, stir the milk, cream and sugar over a low heat until they're combined and all the sugar has dissolved.

2. Bring to the boil, then reduce the heat to a simmer. Stir in the pudding rice and the vanilla seeds and pod. Simmer gently for 45 minutes or until the rice is tender. Stir frequently to stop the rice from sticking to the bottom of the pan.

3. Preheat the grill to a medium heat. Transfer the rice pudding to a heatproof serving dish. Sprinkle the top with 3 tbsp caster sugar and place under the grill until the sugar turns golden and is bubbling.

• Rice To See You •

It wasn't until the 18th century that rice imports became more common and the price started to drop. By the start of the 20th century, rice had become so plentiful and affordable that it was accessible to everyone, not just the elite. It became a cheap meal for the working class that was both warming and filling. It may have been its cheapness that led to rice pudding's downfall though. Served up in industrial quantities in schools and hospitals, many people only had memories of a pudding that was lumpy and tasteless. Thankfully, in recent years, rice pudding has shed this image and made its way back on to our tables. It's the perfect base to experiment with flavours and interesting additions of fruit and nuts. These days, rice pudding flavours are far more exciting than simply stirring through a spoon of jam!

4. Serve the rice pudding warm, drizzled with as much golden syrup as makes you happy!

Gin And Lime Cheesecake

As cocktails became popular in the 1920s and 30s, gin palaces evolved into cocktail and dance venues (think Darby Sabini's Eden Club). Any dessert with gin in cannot fail to whisk you, feathers fluttering and beads jingling, back to this glamorous time.

– INGREDIENTS –
Serves 6

For the base

1 large packet digestive biscuits
(or ginger biscuits give an extra zing)

35g unsalted butter, melted

For the filling

300g marscapone cheese

200ml double cream

1 tbsp caster sugar

1 tbsp icing sugar

50ml gin

2 limes, zest and juice

· The Eden Club ·

Darby Sabini's Eden Club features in the *Peaky Blinders* TV series as a glamorous jazz venue where people went to be seen. The reality is very different. In real life, the club was called the Eden Social Club and was located near Euston Station in London. Far from being an opulent nightspot, it was a two-storey premises above a motor garage with one floor dedicated to card playing!

– METHOD –

1. Line an 18cm round springform tin with greaseproof paper.

2. Crush the biscuits and stir in the melted butter until completely combined. Use the mixture to form the cheesecake base in the tin and then put in the fridge to set.

3. In a bowl, mix together the marscapone and the icing sugar. Slowly and gradually add the gin, taking care not to beat the marscapone too much.

4. In another bowl, whip the cream with the caster sugar until it forms firm peaks.

5. Fold the cream into the marscapone mixture. Add the lime juice a little bit at a time until the flavour is to your taste.

6. Fold in the lime zest, saving some for decoration.

7. Add the filling to the chilled base and leave to set in the fridge for at least 5 hours until firm.

8. Serve sprinkled with the remaining lime zest.

Roobub Pie

Rhubarb has always been popular but when a new variety was introduced in the 1830s, England fell in love with it all over again. Victoria rhubarb was easy to grow and much more sweet and tender than the more tart varieties. The Victorians started to put it in everything! Rhubarb remained hugely popular well into the 1930s and 40s.

– INGREDIENTS –
Serves 8

1 sheet of ready-rolled shortcrust pastry

900g rhubarb, cut into 1cm slices

225g granulated sugar

3 tbsp cornflour

1 egg, beaten, to glaze

1 tbsp caster sugar, to sprinkle on the pie top

– METHOD –

1. Preheat the oven to 180°C/160°C fan/ gas mark 4.

2. In a large bowl, mix together the sugar and cornflour. Stir in the rhubarb until evenly coated.

3. Put the rhubarb filling into a 20cm diameter pie dish. Use a pastry brush to brush some of the beaten egg on the pie dish edge, then cover with the sheet of pastry. Crimp the sides with your fingers to seal them and cut some slits in the top. Chill for 30 minutes in the fridge.

4. After chilling, brush the top of the pie with the remaining beaten egg and sprinkle with the caster sugar.

5. Bake in the oven for 45 minutes to 1 hour, or until the rhubarb is tender and the pastry is golden.

6. Serve hot with custard or ice cream.

· Did You Know? ·

In the 1930s, the repetition of the word 'rhubarb' was first used by stage actors to simulate the murmur of background conversation. The word was chosen because of its lack of distinct phonemes (speech sounds) and whilst it made actors look like they were speaking, what they were saying was indistinguishable and so didn't distract the audience from the main speakers. It's still used to this day.

Rumble and raisin crème brûlée

In the early 1900s, the dining critic John William Severin Gouley wrote that rum makes the most "quarrelsome and pugnacious kind of drink" – perfect for a Peaky Blinder then! If you like rum in your pudding, the range to choose from will leave you spoilt for choice. This recipe combines rum with another favourite from the era – custard.

– INGREDIENTS –
Serves 6

50g raisins

60ml dark rum

625ml whipping cream

7 large egg yolks

100g demerara sugar, plus 6 tsp

– METHOD –

1. Preheat the oven to 170°C/150°C fan/ gas mark 3.

2. In a bowl, mix the raisins with the rum and leave to stand for 30 minutes.

3. In a saucepan, heat the cream until bubbles start to form, then set aside.

4. Whisk the egg yolks and 100g of the sugar together in a bowl and then slowly stir in the warm cream.

5. Stir the liquid from the rum and raisin mixture into the cream. Put the raisins to one side.

6. Place 6 ramekin dishes on a deep baking tray. Divide the raisins between the ramekins and pour the custard mixture over the top. Add hot water to the tray and carefully place in the oven.

7. Bake in the oven for 30–35 minutes or until the centre is set. Put the ramekins on a wire tray to cool for 10 minutes, then place in the fridge until completely chilled.

8. Before serving, sprinkle the top of each custard with a teaspoon of sugar. Use a kitchen torch to caramelise the topping or place under a hot grill until the sugar is crisp and evenly caramelised.

· Rum-Running ·

Rum-running is the illegal business of smuggling alcohol. The term originated in the Prohibition period in the US (1920–1933) when the production, importation, transportation and sale of alcohol was forbidden by law. Cheap rum was smuggled in from the Bahamas to the speakeasies, where it was sold illicitly. In *Peaky Blinders*, Alfie Solomons runs an illegal rum distillery under the cover of a bakery.

Bally Filler – Bread Pudding

Black Country bread pudding was known as a 'bally filler' – a filling, nourishing dish that could sustain families' bellies when they were working long hours. Bread was an important part of people's diets in the late 1800s and early 1900s and bread pudding was a delicious way to make use of stale bread rather than waste it. Britain's love of bread pudding still lives on.

– INGREDIENTS –
Serves 4–6

500g white bread *(fresh or stale)*

500g mixed dried fruit

1½ tbsp mixed spice

600ml milk

3 eggs

140g muscovado sugar

100g unsalted melted butter
(or suet if you want to be more traditional!)

Demerara sugar

– METHOD –

1. Preheat the oven to 180°C/160°C fan/ gas mark 4.

2. Break the bread up into pieces in a large bowl. If using stale bread, soak in water for 15 mins then squeeze out the water. Add the dried fruit, mixed spice and milk and squish it all together with your hands.

3. Beat the eggs and add them to the bowl along with the muscovado sugar and melted butter. Mix until all the ingredients are thoroughly combined.

4. Transfer the mixture to a large ovenproof dish and sprinkle with the demerara sugar.

5. Bake in the oven for 1½ hours until golden brown. Serve cut into squares with custard or ice cream.

• Bread Etiquette •

Did you think that making a sandwich was pretty straightforward? Not if you were living in the 19th or early 20th century! Recipe books and magazines were very specific in their advice about how to go about making a sandwich for lunch. For ladies and children, the bread was supposed to be sliced very thinly and the crusts removed. For workers, thick slices with crusts were deemed more appropriate. Know your place!

Jam Roly-Poly

When it comes to bally-fillers, jam roly-poly – or indeed any suet pudding – is a sure-fire winner. Also known variously as 'shirt-sleeve pudding', 'dead man's arm' or 'dead man's leg', it's a long-standing British classic. Definitely a stodgy pudding, rather than a delicate dessert, so get stuck in.

– INGREDIENTS –
Serves 4–6

15g unsalted butter, plus extra for greasing

175g self-raising flour, plus extra for rolling

Salt

2 tbsp of caster sugar

75g shredded suet

115ml milk, plus extra for brushing

125g strawberry or raspberry jam

– METHOD –

1. Pre-heat the oven to 200°C/180°C fan/ gas mark 6.

2. Cut a 30cm-long piece of baking paper and grease one side with butter. Make a pleat along the middle of the baking paper, lengthwise, to let the roly-poly expand.

3. Sift the flour and salt into a bowl and use your fingertips to rub in the butter. Add the sugar and suet and stir until the ingredients are thoroughly combined.

4. Add the milk and mix to make a firm dough. Roll out on a floured surface to form a 22cm x 30cm rectangle. Spread one side with jam, leaving a 1.5cm-wide border. Brush the border with milk and then roll up the dough from the short end (like a Swiss roll).

5. Put the roly-poly onto the greased side of the baking paper and loosely roll the paper up. Then wrap it loosely in foil, sealing the edges.

6. Fill a deep roasting tin half way up with boiling water. Place a wire rack on the roasting tin to create a bain-marie. Put the roly-poly on the rack, but make sure the water doesn't touch the foil. Bake for 45 minutes.

7. Unwrap the roly-poly, slice and serve hot. Perfect with custard!

· School Dinners ·

Jam roly-poly has long been a favourite feature of British school dinners. Back in 1900, despite efforts to improve public health and housing, children were no healthier than they had been in the 1840s. Britain's Liberal government elected in 1906 tried to address this by encouraging schools to provide meals. The first school meals were stodgy but also quite tasty and included dishes such as mutton stew, toad in the hole and fish and potato pie. By the time the First World War began, 14 million lunches were being served in schools.

Maple, Whiskey And Bacon Cupcakes

These aren't strictly Blinder food nor do they hail from the Black Country, but we think that if they did they'd be a Shelby family favourite. Why? Whiskey, of course. And the bacon – this is a sweet and naughty alternative to eating it with Grey Peas.

– INGREDIENTS –
Makes 20

For the cupcakes
150g unsalted butter, softened

100g brown sugar

50g caster sugar

3 eggs

190g plain flour

1½ tsp baking powder

60ml milk

60ml whiskey

1 tsp vanilla extract

For the buttercream
500g icing sugar

250g unsalted butter, softened

6-8 tbsp maple syrup

Sea salt, to taste

For the candied bacon
5 rashers streaky bacon

Maple syrup

– METHOD –

1. Preheat the oven to 180°C/160°C fan/ gas mark 4.

2. In a bowl, beat the butter, brown sugar and caster sugar together until light and fluffy.

3. Add all the remaining cupcake ingredients and beat until the mixture is smooth and creamy.

4. Spoon the mixture into paper cupcake cases. Bake in the oven for 18–20 minutes, or until a skewer comes out clean when inserted in a cupcake. Leave to cool for a few minutes and then transfer to a wire tray.

5. Increase the oven temperature to 200°C/180°C fan/gas mark 4. Brush both sides of the bacon with maple syrup and place on a baking tray. Cook the bacon in the oven until crispy and caramelised. Set aside to cool.

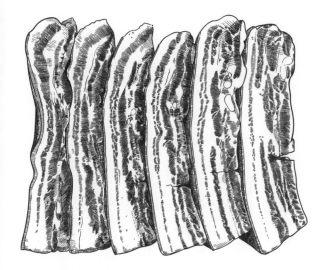

6. To make the buttercream icing, cream the butter in a bowl until soft and fluffy. Add the icing sugar and mix until combined. Finally, stir in the maple syrup until it becomes smooth and creamy. Add the syrup slowly (you may not need all of it) so that the buttercream doesn't become runny. Sprinkle in the sea salt and mix again.

7. Pipe the buttercream onto the cupcakes and top with a sliver of the caramelised bacon!

• Butter Wouldn't Melt ...? •

These cupcakes may well have brought out the softer side of the Peaky Blinders – but because of the age of the gang members, not the whiskey. Whilst in the TV series the gang members are adults, in real life the Blinders were teens and tweens, some even as young as 12 years old. Perhaps if the police had put on a spread of cakes and sweets they could have lured in and rounded up the offenders more easily!

Gooseberry Nobody's Fool

The gooseberry was one of the first fruits ever cultivated commercially in Britain. Back in the 1900s, many houses with gardens would have had a gooseberry bush. In the Midlands and the North of England, these hairy berries were adored and a tradition of competitive growing developed – basically, who could grow the heaviest gooseberry! No doubt there were some 'friendly' fights.

– INGREDIENTS –
Serves 6

450g gooseberries

100g caster sugar

200ml milk

1 egg

2 tsp cornflour

1 tsp vanilla essence

150ml double cream

· Did You Know? ·

A 'gooseberry picker' used to be the name used for a thief who specialised in stealing clothes from washing lines! Expert 'knickers' but sounds like a pants line of work nonetheless!

– METHOD –

1. Top and tail the gooseberries and gently rub off any hairs. Put the gooseberries into a saucepan and add half the sugar. Simmer over a gentle heat until the gooseberries are tender. Puree in a blender and then set aside to cool.

2. To make the custard, start by warming the milk in a saucepan. In a bowl, whisk the egg together with the cornflour, remaining sugar and vanilla essence. Pour in the warm milk, whisking continuously. Return the mixture to the milk pan, heating gently, and whisk until thickened. Remove from the heat just as it starts to boil and set aside to cool.

3. Whip the double cream until it forms soft peaks. Fold the gooseberry puree into the cooled custard and then fold in the cream. Chill before serving in glasses.

Rascally Rice Pudding Sponge Cake

Another Black Country favourite to well and truly line your stomach for a night out at The Garrison?! Of course. This recipe is a slightly lighter version of the traditional one, using vegetable shortening instead of suet and therefore leaving more room for Whiskey Scuffles (see page 79) with your coffee.

– INGREDIENTS –
Serves 4–6

100g ground rice

100g plain flour

100g vegetable shortening, eg. Trex

50g brown sugar

150g raisins

1 tsp bicarbonate of soda

235ml milk

Pinch of salt

– METHOD –

1. In a large bowl, mix together all the dry ingredients until combined thoroughly.

2. Slowly add the milk to the bowl of dry ingredients, mixing as you go.

3. Grease a 2-pint (1.2 litre) pudding basin and fill with the pudding mixture.

4. Cover the pudding basin with a piece of greaseproof paper and secure with string. Place the basin in a large stock pot and fill with water until two-thirds of the basin is covered. Put a lid on the pot and boil for 2 hours (or until a cocktail stick comes out of the pudding clean). Check the water levels whilst cooking and add more water if necessary.

5. Serve with custard – what else?!

· A New Brand Of Gangster ·

Since the *Peaky Blinders* TV series has been on our screens and the huge increase in interest in the real gangs behind the story, Blinder-branded food and drink has appeared on shelves everywhere. You can buy Peaky Blinder whiskey, rum, gin, cheese (yes, cheese!), beer, pizza, burgers and chocolate. Would you like gangster milk with your gangster cereal, sir/madam?

'Eden Club' Mess

What is peakier than a meringue?! Get whisking up those razor-sharp peaks to create this glorious English summer dessert. 'Eton' mess was first mentioned in 1893 and originated from Eton College, where it was served at the annual cricket match against Harrow School and was available well into the 1930s in the school's tuck shop.

– INGREDIENTS –
Serves 8

For the meringue

4 egg whites

200g caster sugar

For the mess

450ml double cream

400g mixed berries, e.g. strawberries, raspberries, blueberries

– METHOD –

1. Preheat the oven to 120°C/100°C fan/ gas mark ½. Line a baking tray with baking parchment.

2. To make the meringue: in a bowl, whisk the egg whites until stiff. You should be able to turn the bowl upside down without the mixture falling out!

3. Gradually whisk in the caster sugar until the mixture is shiny. Spread onto the baking tray. Try to keep it around 1cm thick but it doesn't need to be neat and tidy.

4. Cook the meringue in the oven for 3 hours.

5. To make the mess: in a bowl, whisk the cream until it is stiff and forms peaks. Spoon into the serving dish (or individual dishes).

6. Break the cooked meringue into random chunks and gently mix them into the cream. Finally, add the berries and carefully combine so as not to squish the berries. It needs to be messy but not that messy!

· The 1920s – The Golden · Age Of Nightclubs

In 1921, the law had changed to allow alcohol to be served until 12.30am, provided food was also available. Nightclubs were decadent, exciting and expensive and were the places to go to be seen and to dance the night away. Popular dances included the Job-rot, Shimmy and Heebie-Jeebie, all with the backdrop of the new jazz bands (and the occasional police raid!).

Wicked Whiskey Pound Cake

This sounds like a thug of a cake that, if thrown in your direction, might cause a serious injury. It is indeed a mighty cake and the name comes from the weight of each of the ingredients traditionally used to make it. With a splash of whiskey, this is sure to go down a treat with your band of hungry gangsters.

– INGREDIENTS –

225g butter, softened

225g sugar

6 eggs

225g self-raising flour, sifted

1 tsp salt

¼ tsp ground cinnamon

¼ tsp ground nutmeg

250ml sour cream

2 tbsp whiskey

125g chopped walnuts

For the glaze

250g icing sugar

2 tbsp whiskey

3 tbsp water

· First World War Rationing ·

At the end of 1917, food was being sent from Britain to the soldiers fighting the war and less and less was being imported into the country. People were scared that food would run out and started panic buying (sound anything like the Great Corona virus Toilet Roll Shortage of early 2020?!). In 1918, the government introduced rationing so that everyone got what they needed – this included sugar, meat, flour, butter and milk. Extra rations were allowed for 'arduous work', however, according to the brilliant Black Country Living Museum, whilst this extended to postmen, it didn't apply to postwomen!

– METHOD –

1. Preheat the oven to 170°C/150°C fan/gas mark 3. Grease and line a 25cm cake tin.

2. In a large bowl, cream the butter until light and fluffy. Gradually stir in the sugar. Add the eggs and beat until smooth.

3. Sift in the flour, salt, cinnamon and nutmeg. Beat in the sour cream and whiskey until completely blended and then fold in the walnuts.

4. Transfer to the cake tin and bake in the oven for around 1 hour 30 minutes, or until a skewer inserted in the centre comes out clean. Leave to cool.

5. To make the glaze, mix the icing sugar and whiskey with a little bit of water. The glaze should be pourable but not too runny. Drizzle over the cake and leave to set.

Rock Cakes

Stalwarts of the English table, these teatime favourites are named after their craggy appearance rather than their ability to knock out a member of a rival gang at ten paces. The first known recipe for rock cakes appeared in Mrs Beeton's *Book of Household Management* in 1861. Given that she recommended cooking carrots by boiling them for two hours, 'rock biscuits' was hopefully one of her better recipes!

– INGREDIENTS –

225g plain flour

½ tsp salt

2 tsp baking powder

85g unsalted butter

85g caster sugar

1 egg

115g mixed dried fruit

2 tbsp milk

– METHOD –

1. Preheat the oven to 230°C/210°C fan/gas mark 8. Line a baking tray with greaseproof paper.

2. In a large bowl, mix together the flour, baking powder and salt. Using your fingers, rub in the butter until the mixture looks like breadcrumbs. Add the sugar and mix.

3. Add the egg and dried fruit. Pour in the milk and mix together until it all forms a stiff mixture. Add more milk if the mixture is too dry but avoid adding too much and making it sloppy.

4. Using a spoon, shape the mixture into 10 heaps on the baking tray. Bake for 10–15 minutes. Cool on a wire rack to let them firm up. Enjoy with lashings of butter.

• Throwing A Wobbly •

Whilst the British were preserving their gooseberries and fighting each other in peaked caps, an iconic dessert was being born in the US. In 1897, a man named Pearle Bixby Wait trademarked a gelatine-based dessert called Jell-O. By 1902, it was being marketed as 'America's Most Famous Dessert'. By the 1920s, Jell-O was found in pretty much every American home. In the 1930s, Jell-O started to cash in on the passion for preserving anything in aspic – including salads. Today, more than 420 million boxes of Jell-O are sold in the US every year!

Whiskey Scuffles

If you make it to after dinner coffee without lamping each other, impress your guests with these bostin' truffles made with one of the Peaky Blinders' favourite tipples.

– INGREDIENTS –

200g dark chocolate, finely chopped

200g double cream

2 tbsp whiskey
(the Blinders prefer Irish single malt)

100g dark chocolate flakes

'Whiskey is good proofing water. It tells you who's real and who isn't.'
TOMMY SHELBY

– METHOD –

1. Bring the cream to the boil in a large saucepan. Take off the heat and add 150g of the chopped chocolate. Leave to melt for a few minutes, then gently stir until the chocolate and cream mixture is smooth. Stir in the whiskey.

2. Place the mixture in the fridge for 30 minutes to firm up.

3. When firm, roll the mixture into small truffle-sized balls. Put back in the fridge for a further 30 minutes.

4. Melt the remaining chopped chocolate gently in a bowl placed over hot (not boiling) water. Make sure the bowl doesn't touch the water.

5. Scatter the chocolate flakes on a large plate or a shallow dish. Using a fork, pick up the balls of mixture and dip them in the melted chocolate. Then roll them in the chocolate flakes until coated.

6. Leave in a cool place to set. They should be fully set in around an hour.

Coconut Tapioca Pudding

Poor old tapioca pudding. Lumped together with rice pudding (pun intended), tapioca is another victim of the time when school dinners in Britain were pretty terrible. Most school children who endured it will remember it as the 'frog spawn' that was served from massive metal bowls. If you want to experience how truly tasty tapioca actually is, don't buy it ready-prepared in tins – make your own from scratch. This light and refreshing dessert will completely wipe your memory of tadpoles ...

– INGREDIENTS –
Serves 4

60g small pearl tapioca

640ml coconut milk

60g granulated sugar

¼ tsp salt

½ tsp vanilla extract

Sliced fresh fruit, such as mango, melon or pineapple

Coconut flakes, to garnish

– METHOD –

1. Put the tapioca and coconut milk in a medium-sized saucepan and leave to soak for 30 minutes.

2. Add the sugar and salt to the saucepan and heat gently until it starts to simmer. Reduce the heat and continue to simmer for 15 minutes, until the tapioca pearls are transparent and the mixture has thickened up. Stir regularly to stop the tapioca from sticking to the bottom of the pan. Remove from the heat and then stir in the vanilla extract.

3. Pour the mixture into small serving dishes. Put the dishes in the fridge for at least 3 hours or until completely chilled and the mixture has thickened up.

4. Serve with your choice of sliced fresh fruit. Sprinkle with coconut flakes.

· Why The 'Black Country'? ·

It seems that the young queen-to-be Victoria is to blame for the name! At the age of 13, on a visit to Wolverhampton and Birmingham, she wrote in her diary:

"The men, woemen [sic], children, country and houses are all black. But I can not by any description give an idea of its strange and extraordinary appearance.

"The country is very desolate every where; there are coals about, and the grass is quite blasted and black. I just now see an extraordinary building flaming with fire. The country continues black, engines flaming, coals, in abundance, every where, smoking and burning coal heaps, intermingled with wretched huts and carts and little ragged children."

Apple Snow

This is a simple recipe that's incredibly delicious. It's an old-fashioned pudding and it first appeared in a recipe book around 1886. Use your imagination and it's easy to picture a cook in a Victorian kitchen whipping it up to serve to the family and their guests. Mention the recipe to someone of a certain age and they're likely to say they remember their grandmother making it.

– INGREDIENTS –
Serves 4

750g Bramley cooking apples (peeled, cored and cut into small pieces)

100g caster sugar

Grated zest of 1 lemon

3 tbsp lemon juice

2 egg whites

100ml double cream

1 small red eating apple

4 sprigs mint

· Apples At The Core Of · The West Midlands

Bulmers has been producing cider in Herefordshire in the West Midlands since 1887, when Percy Bulmer first pressed apples from his father's orchard. Percy's father was a keen amateur cidermaker who was persuaded by his wife to devote his energy to bringing it to market: "Food and drink never go out of fashion," she said wisely. The company is now the world's leading cider maker. They were granted the Royal Warrant in 1911 and have held it ever since. Bulmers has the largest apple pressing mill in the world and they meet over 60% of the UK's demand for cider.

– METHOD –

1. Add the Bramley apples to a large saucepan with 50g of the sugar, the lemon zest and 2 tbsp of the lemon juice. Cover and cook over a medium heat, stirring, until the apples are soft.

2. Cook for a few minutes, without the lid on, stirring. Transfer into a large bowl and mash with a fork. Set aside until cold.

3. Whisk the egg whites until they're stiff. Add the remaining sugar and whisk again until stiff.

4. In a separate bowl, whisk the cream until it starts to hold its shape.

5. Fold the egg whites and cream into the apples and divide between four serving glasses. Put in the fridge to chill.

6. Core the red eating apple. Cut into thin slices and toss in the remaining lemon juice.

7. To serve, top each serving glass with apple slices and mint.

Black Country Remedies

The NHS wasn't founded until 1948, so what would you have done if you were ill and the boss expected you down the racecourse checking rival gangs weren't poaching your business? Natural remedies! Some of these will sound a bit bonkers to us modern-day types who are used to heading to the chemist or GP with our aches and pains.

Here are some interesting remedies, featured in *Bostin' Fittle* (1978) by Pat Purcell, inspired by Miss Bissell's 1875 recipe notebook. Just remember this warning from the author: "Most of these are included for their curiosity value and should be treated with caution."

– ELIXIR VITAE – ('ELIXIR OF LIFE')

Break 6 eggs into a jug with their shells and beat. Add the juice from 6 lemons. Mix and leave for 3 days then strain. Boil 227g sugar in 275ml water until the sugar dissolves. Add 570ml rum. Add the egg mixture to the sugar, water and rum mixture. And the best bit ... have a wineglassful after breakfast!!

– HICCUPS –

Swallow a teaspoonful of sugar soaked in vinegar or lemon juice. Or try holding one arm outstretched. Left arm for right-handed people, right arm for left-handed people!

– FLATULENCE –

Toast two slices of bread until they are burnt. Break them into pieces in a bowl and cover with boiling water. Drink when cooled.

– STIFF NECK –

After you take your socks off at night, wrap one of them loosely around your neck. Wonder if it's the warmth or the smell that provides the relief?

– WARTS –

Rub the wart with the sap from a dandelion stem. Sprinkle on salt water and sand and cover with a plaster. Put your own saliva on it several times a day and, finally, pop on some witch hazel.

– EARACHE –

Wrap two large onions in greaseproof paper and bake in the oven until soft. Remove the centre cores of the baked onions and place them in the ear. Oh no no no ...

Drinks At
The Garrison

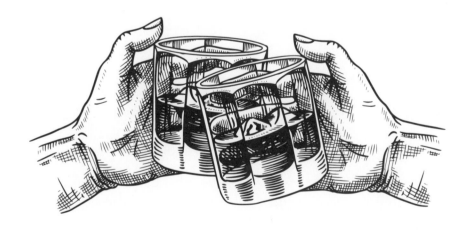

Lambswool

If you were asked to guess what this drink was, you'd probably be flummoxed. Lambswool, also known as 'Wassail', was traditionally drunk on Twelfth Night. It gets its name because the frothy pulp of the roasted apples looks like fluffy lamb's wool. The drink gets a specific mention in a folklore guide to Birmingham and the Midlands but was consumed in other areas of England too.

– INGREDIENTS –

2.25l dry cider

15g ginger root, peeled

6 cloves

1 blade of mace

1 tsp ground nutmeg

½ tsp ground coriander

4 cardamom pods

225g granulated sugar

2 lemons

275ml water

2 egg yolks

Demerara sugar

6 small cooking apples

– METHOD –

1. Use a hammer to bruise the ginger. Put the ginger into a large pan with the cloves, nutmeg, mace, coriander, cardamom and sugar.

2. Grate the rinds of the lemons and add the zest to the spices with the water.

3. Bring the pan to the boil and simmer for 5 minutes.

4. Squeeze the lemons and add the juice to the pan along with the cider. Heat the mixture slowly.

5. Place the egg yolks in a large bowl and slowly beat in 235ml of the liquid from the pan. The mixture in the bowl should go frothy. When the remaining mixture in the pan comes to the boil, pour it into the basin with the egg mixture and whisk.

6. Preheat the oven to 190°C/170°C fan/gas mark 5. Core the apples and place them in a roasting tin. Fill the cored centres with demerara sugar and then bake in the oven for 20 minutes. Peel the hot apples and either whisk the flesh into a mush or pop it in a blender. Stir the apple mush into the large basin.

7. Your lambswool is complete. Enjoy whilst dancing around a tree!

Elderflower Champagne

This might sound like a fancy champagne cocktail you'd only drink in your 1920s finery, but in fact it's a low-cost concoction that you can easily make for yourself from scratch. It is low in alcohol but it's not non-alcoholic so remember that when you're riding home from The Garrison on your horse. It's best to pick the elderflowers in the morning when they smell of bananas, rather than in the afternoon and evening when they tend to smell of cat wee!

– INGREDIENTS –

10 elderflower heads

540g caster sugar

2 tbsp white wine vinegar

6l cold water
(bottled rather than tap water ideally)

2 large lemons zested and juiced

– METHOD –

1. Pick the elderflowers when they're fully in flower. The best time to find them is normally June. Shake to remove any creepy crawlies. Don't wash them as they need to be dry.

2. In a large, clean container, dissolve the sugar in half of the water (warm). When the sugar has dissolved, add the rest of the water.

3. When the water has cooled, add the vinegar, lemon juice and zest. Stir to mix and then add the elderflowers.

4. Seal the container and leave to stand for 72 hours. You should see some froth or bubbles appear from the natural fermentation process. If you don't see any froth after a day, add a pinch of yeast.

5. After 3 days, remove the flowers and strain into strong glass screw-top bottles. Leave somewhere cool for 2 weeks. Make sure you release the fizz every couple of days or the bottles might explode.

6. Serve chilled with a slice of lemon and a sprig of mint. (If you don't drink it all at once and are storing it, remember to regularly check the pressure build up so the bottles don't burst!)

• A Little Something Extra •

If you find you like your elderflowers alcoholic, then try making elderflower gin. It's quick, easy and doesn't require any cooking. There's no excuse not to, really! Snip between 12 and 18 elderflower heads into a large jar with two tablespoons of caster sugar and a litre of gin. Seal the jar and give it a swirl twice a day to dissolve the sugar. After 3 days, strain the mixture into bottles through a muslin-lined sieve. It's as easy as that. And the taste of summer is out of this world! Try adding some lavender too.

Classic Martini

Probably the most famous gin cocktail of them all. Elegant, sharp and dry – rather like a Peaky Blinder aspires to … until they get caught up in a ruckus. And into the bargain, you get a pre-dinner snack – an olive. It's thought that the martini originated in the 1860s; by the 1920s it was one of the most popular drinks to sip as you Charlestoned your way across the nightclub.

– INGREDIENTS –
Serve in a … martini glass!

50ml gin

15ml dry vermouth

Zest of a lemon

A couple of green olives

• The Gin Craze •

The first half of the 18th century saw the Gin Craze in Britain, a time of drunken havoc across the country but primarily in London. In London alone there were around 7,000 gin shops by 1730. For the working classes, gin was a drink that kept them warm, staved off hunger pangs and made for a welcome escape from a miserable life in the slums. Unfortunately, drunkenness, violence and addiction were by-products of the Gin Craze.

In the 19th century, the notorious gin shops were being replaced by glamorous new gin palaces where you'd simply buy and down a shot and leave – a bit like an alcoholic espresso bar. In the second half of the century, gin was steadily becoming popular as an ingredient in cocktails. Gin reached heady heights of popularity in the 1920s and was THE spirit to be served at upmarket parties.

– METHOD –

1. Pour the gin and dry vermouth in a cocktail shaker with ice. Stir well – don't shake it as you want to treat it gently and prevent it from clouding.

2. Strain into a chilled martini glass – ideally a glass that has been in the freezer.

3. Now garnish stylishly! Peel off a strip of lemon zest and twist it into a spiral. Hang on the side of the glass. Finally, put your olives on a cocktail stick and float them in the glass.

Head Of Industrial Steam

What would a Peaky Blinder drink be without whiskey? Not worthy of associating with the Shelbys, that's what! This simple recipe is sure to get you going. Think of the gangs striding through the flames and smoke of the backstreets of Brum … and then imagine that going off in your head. Spicy, sweet and a little on the naughty side, this one gives a Shelby girl a run for her money.

– INGREDIENTS –

45ml Irish whiskey

30ml vermouth

15ml sweet sherry

4 dashes bitters

4 dashes Mexican chocolate bitters

Orange peel oil

– METHOD –

1. Add all the ingredients into a mixing glass with ice. Stir.

2. Strain into a chilled glass. A tulip, goblet or wine glass are perfect.

3. Squeeze some oil from a piece of orange peel on the top.

· Irish Whiskey: · Did You Know?

More mellow than bourbon and more affordable than Scotch, Irish whiskey goes down your cakehole much more easily. It's smooth, warm and slightly sweet, with a hint of caramel.

If you want to impress your cockers, don't ask for an Irish whiskey with ice ('on the rocks', or 'on the ropes' if you're a bareknuckle fighter). Adding anything that detracts from the flavour is seen as sacrilege. Of course, you need to forget that ice advice when you're mixing cocktails.

In June 1875, rivers of burning whiskey flowed through the streets of Dublin like lava after a whiskey warehouse caught fire. The Great Dublin Whiskey Fire took the lives of 13 people and 1,900 barrels of whiskey were lost.

The world's most expensive bottle of Irish whiskey is a 25-year-old Pure Pot Still Whiskey dating back to the late 1800s. It is one of the last to be produced at a distillery in Galway, which closed in 1913. If you'd like to buy the bottle, your racketeering and illegal betting business better be doing well – it will cost you £100,000!

Eden Club Fizz

"It is merely a rendezvous of pickpockets and thieves, accessible only to a chosen few. I feel sure you will enjoy yourselves there, for the bartender has the secret of a remarkable gin fizz, sweeter than a maiden's smile, more intoxicating than a kiss."

Rex Beach, in his 1911 novel *The Ne'er-Do-Well,* could well have been talking about the real-life Eden Club (see page 67). Although we're sure Charles Sabini would disagree quite vigorously! This cocktail is a 19th century take on Pink Gin – it's sweeter than the original Eden Club version but just as decadent as the fictional club in *Peaky Blinders*.

– INGREDIENTS –

50ml gin

10ml lemon juice

5ml grenadine or raspberry syrup

10ml sweet vermouth

Handful fresh raspberries

1 egg white

Raspberry to garnish

– METHOD –

1. Dry shake (i.e. without ice) all the ingredients together until the egg white has fully mixed in and the raspberries are pulverised (as if they've been scragging with a Blinder).

2. Add half a cup of ice to the mixture.

3. Get shekin' again until it's cold.

4. Strain into a glass and you're ready to go.

5. Serve in a coupe glass (also known as a champagne saucer) with a raspberry on top to garnish.

• Prohibition •

Around the time the Peaky Blinders *et al* were making their mark (mainly on other people's faces), the United States implemented a ban that prevented alcohol from being made, transported or sold. Prohibition was established in 1920 and remained in force for 13 years. One of the reasons for Prohibition was alcohol's association with criminality. But of course, Prohibition was a golden opportunity for gangsters to make money from bootleg alcohol. Rival gang warfare became rife; in Chicago alone, it's claimed there were 729 gangland killings between 1919 and 1933.

Drink Whiskey Like A Peaky Blinder

The Peaky Blinders are brilliant at two things: crime and drinking whiskey. Want to impress a girl? Drink whiskey. Need to negotiate a shady deal? Drink whiskey. The Blinders know that whiskey is a tipple for all occasions and all company (whether friend or foe).

—

Make it Irish whiskey.

—

Drink it neat. All those flames in the neighbourhood would melt any ice anyway.

—

Look stylish: try brooding menacingly or simply stare at your glass like it holds the answer to who to make an enemy of next.

—

Don't clart about: make your measures generous and keep your guests' glasses full.

—

Black Country And Brummie Slang

One of the great things about there being so many distinct regions in Britain is that the informal language and slang varies from place to place. If you find yourself in Birmingham or the Black Country, try some of these (mostly) food-related sayings.

Bostin': Amazing, brilliant or excellent.

"This is the most bostin' meal I've ever eaten."

Bab: An affectionate term for 'love' or 'dear'.

"Would you like custard with your bread pudding, bab?"

Chobbling: Munching loudly.

"Can you please eat that pikelet without chobbling?!"

Clarting about: Messing about.

Cob: Bread roll (as it resembles a cobblestone).

Fittle: Food.

Graunching: Crunching loudly when eating.

Klondikes: Fried slices of potato from the chip shop (also known as **scallops**).

"Klondikes with lashings of curry sauce, please."

Never in a rain of pigs pudding: Something that will never happen.

"A Peaky Blinder in a Hawaiian shirt? Never in a rain of pig's pudding!"

Oil tot: When someone feels satisfied and happy. Refers to when men would have a swig of olive oil before drinking beer, believing that it would line their stomachs and stop them getting too drunk.

Outdoor: Off-licence.

Piece: A slice of bread and butter, sometimes also used to mean 'sandwich'.

"Can I get you a piece with your soup?"

Pop: Any fizzy soft drink.

Rocks: Hard sweets.

"Graunch any harder and those rocks will break yer teeth."

Snap: Food or a meal.

Wassin: Throat.

"Gerrit down yer wassin!" **("Eat/drink it!")**

Wench: Affectionate term for a young girl or woman.

"Another whiskey please, wench!"
(But perhaps don't try this one in a restaurant or pub!)

Plots And Plans

- RECIPE NOTES -

Plots And Plans

- RECIPE NOTES -

Plots And Plans

- RECIPE NOTES -